Becoming
a Man *of*
Unwavering
Faith

WITH COMMENTARY AND A FOREWORD BY

Joel Osteen

Becoming a Man *of* Unwavering Faith

JOHN OSTEEN

New York | Boston | Nashville

Literary development and design: Koechel Peterson & Assoc., Inc., Mpls., MN

FaithWords
Hachette Book Group
237 Park Avenue, New York, NY 10017
Visit our Web site at www.faithwords.com.

The FaithWords name and logo are trademarks of Hachette Book Group, USA.

Printed in the United States of America.

First Printing: April 2011

10 9 8 7 6 5 4 3 2 1

ISBN: 9780892968893

LCCN: 2001012345

CONTENTS

WHEN I WAS YOUNG, I often heard my father tell our church congregation, "I want you to look out there with me today and see that brand-new sanctuary." At the time, we were meeting in a small rundown building. But Daddy would say, "I want you to see that new building completed and paid off." People who were visiting with us that particular Sunday probably thought we were crazy. But Daddy would say, "Close your eyes and see that new church sanctuary with me through your eyes of faith. See it full of people worshiping God." We saw that sanctuary many years before it ever came to pass. And today the sixteen-thousand-seat arena of Lakewood Church in Houston has four services each weekend.

That was just who my dad was—a man of faith whose life and ministry were shaped through adversity and great challenges. As you read this book, you'll see exactly what I mean, and I have no doubt that you'll be inspired by his message.

The beauty of my father's life was that he was a man of great integrity. For me, that means he was the same at home as he was in the church and whenever he was in front of other people. His sincerity had a tremendous impact on me and my siblings, and I'm sure it's a significant reason why today all five of us are working in the ministry.

Daddy was a constant source of inspiration to us. As a boy, he grew up in Great Depression-era poverty with next to nothing. He told me later in his life that "having been raised in that poverty with nothing to eat at times and holes in my pants and shoes, I determined in my heart that my children would never experience the same." For us to watch his determination and faith in God set the whole tone for our lives.

My father was also an incredible example of kindness and compassion for others. He had such a big heart for people. It didn't matter who someone was, whether he or she was rich or poor, up or down, my father was for them. He always believed in the best about people, and he would try to draw that out of them.

My dad's whole message was that you can rise higher, you can overcome, and with God all things are possible. But he didn't just talk about it. He lived it out before us, and for more than forty years he pastored Lakewood Church with great love and faithfulness.

At the end of every chapter, I have added a short personal reflection. I trust that this book will help you unlock doors that lead you to becoming a man of unwavering faith. No matter where you are or what challenges you face, you can start to enjoy a new life as you are transformed and renewed by God's Word!

HE WAS A MAN OF FAITH

whose life and ministry were shaped

through adversity and great challenges.

INTRODUCTION

EVERY MAN FACES STRUGGLES and temptations. There are moments when every man feels surrounded by trouble on every side. Overwhelmed.

Unfortunately, many men become convinced that their destiny is to suffer pain, disease, troubles, anxieties, and defeat. Some resign themselves to the position that nothing can be done about their situation.

The Bible says, "In the world you will have tribulation" (John 16:33). The time will come, if it hasn't already, when you're going to have to believe God for something significant—for your marriage, your finances, your children, your spiritual growth, your health. You need to know how to come to Him in unwavering faith and how to stand on the Word of God.

My own personal journey to becoming a man of faith began as a boy on a cotton farm with five siblings during the Great Depression. As a child, I thought about God many times, but I grew up into my teens having gone to church very little. My best friend, Sam Martin, constantly told me about the love of God, but I wouldn't listen to him and chose to leave Jesus out of my life.

At the age of seventeen, I found myself without peace in my heart. One night while walking home alone from a nightclub in Ft. Worth, Texas, at two o'clock in the morning, I began to think about time . . . eternity . . . heaven. *Where would I spend eternity?* When I got home, I pulled out our old family Bible and came upon a beautiful picture of Jesus standing at a door knocking. Under the picture were the words: "Behold, I stand at the door and knock. If anyone hears My voice and opens the door, I will come in to him and dine with him, and he with Me" (Revelation 3:20). I could understand opening the door of my life and letting Jesus in, so early the next morning I called Sam, and he invited me to go to church with him.

That Sunday morning, I beat Sam to the church! Although I didn't understand the sermon that morning, I had come to give my heart to Jesus, and that was what I was waiting to do. However, when the pastor invited anyone who wanted to receive salvation to come to the front of the church and the invitation song began, it felt as though my shoes were nailed to the floor. I couldn't get the courage to move. Finally, Sam slipped his arm around my shoulder and whispered he'd come with me.

When I got to the front of the church, the pastor asked me if I wanted to receive Jesus in my heart, and I said, "I don't know. I've been real wicked." He shook my hand real hard and said, "I didn't ask you that. Will you receive Jesus as your Savior?" I balked and said, "I don't know. I work in the wrong kind of place." He nearly shook my hand off as he said, "I didn't ask you that. Will you accept Jesus into your heart as your personal Savior?" It was then that I surrendered all to Jesus and said courageously, "Absolutely!" With that word, I passed from death into life, became a new creature in Christ Jesus, and took my first step to becoming a man of faith.

From that day, things were different. My grades in high school went from Cs and Ds to As and Bs. That first year I began preaching anywhere I was welcomed—Bible study groups, nursing homes, and missions. Eventually, I worked my way through college and seminary and became a pastor.

For nineteen years, I ministered in all the knowledge I had and was the pastor of a successful, growing church. But I knew that I had not experienced and was not enjoying the things the believers did in the New Testament, and deep within me I felt God had more for me. One day, with God's help and the prayers of others, I received the baptism in the Holy Spirit and experienced the power of God, which revolutionized me and my ministry.

On Mother's Day 1959, we founded Lakewood Church with ninety members. Over the years, the church grew, and we built an 8,200-seat sanctuary in the middle of the recession in 1988 a few weeks before Christmas—debt free. By 1999, we had 10,000 members. During my ministry, I had the privilege of traveling extensively throughout the world, taking the message of God's love and power to people of all nations, which included making over forty mission trips to India. For sixteen years I hosted my own weekly television program, reaching millions in the U.S. and in many other countries with the Gospel. My books, cassettes, and videotaped messages went all over the world.

The principles of faith in God and His Word set forth in this book have been tried in the crucible of my life. I remember when the doctor told us that our baby daughter Lisa had brain damage and would never be normal. She had no sucking reflexes, no muscle tone, and symptoms similar to cerebral palsy. It was the miracle of her healing that opened my eyes to the miracle-working power of

God and the power of the Holy Spirit.

I remember the time when my nervous system collapsed, and I lost all sense of purpose, direction, and initiative. I felt that life held no hope of reality. I came under a dark hole of fear that God was no longer with me, and I could not sleep. When day came, I wished for night. When night came, I wished for day. God graciously delivered me from that condition, not instantly, but through trusting His Word the victory came.

Some years later, I went through months of agonizing pain in my back and legs and faced back surgery and visions of being paralyzed and unable to walk. Another battle came in 1986 when I was in Methodist Hospital, awaiting open heart surgery. In both situations, Jesus brought me through to victory, permeating my whole being with faith and assurance as I read and believed His Word!

It was in the midst of the great challenges of my life that I learned how to exercise my faith. The Lord Jesus worked in my life and my family through all these conflicts and many more. Through His grace and strength, the fields of battle became my greatest victory ground. Now when fear knocks at my door, faith answers. I learned the power of faith to help me stand and overcome.

So what makes the difference between living a life of victory and faith or living one of defeat and unbelief? What are the qualities of a man of genuine faith? I believe they are exemplified by the lives of the great men of faith in the Bible, particularly Jabez and Elijah and others on whom I will focus in this book.

We are privileged to live in a generation when God is pouring out His Spirit in a mighty way. The gentle rain of the precious Holy Spirit is falling upon the dry religious ground of our day to give sweet refreshing to weary-hearted men of God. He can do it for you . . . today.

The Lord said in the Book of Joel, "I will restore . . ." He is restoring to His Church the power and love of God, and His will is that we become men of faith who bring His presence into the lives of our families and the world around us.

To become a man of unwavering faith, you must first find out what the Word of God says about it, and then do what the Word says to do to obtain it. As you read through the pages of this book, meditate on the biblical truths and crown Jesus as Lord of your life. Trust the Holy Spirit to be your Teacher as you read.

Please do not give up! God's Word works. Jesus loves you! If you heed the message of this book, God will give you light on how to be the man of faith He desires you to be.

THE PRINCIPLES OF FAITH IN GOD...

have been tried in the crucible of his life.

Reflections from
JOEL

On Mother's Day 1959, my father and mother opened Lakewood Church in a rundown building with holes in the floor. For nearly thirteen years that tiny congregation hardly grew at all. It was an extremely dry season in my father's life. He had gone from speaking to thousands of people to laboring in obscurity. But God was doing a work in my father, and those years were a time of testing. Daddy knew if he remained faithful in the tough times, God would promote him, which is exactly what happened. Millions of people have been touched through the ministry of Lakewood Church.

When you go through a long period of time when you don't see anything good happening, just stay faithful; keep a smile on your face, and keep doing what you know is right. God is preparing you for greater things.

CHAPTER ONE

A Man *of* Faith Can Change His Destiny

In the Old Testament is a somewhat obscure man who overcame what appeared to be a destiny that included pain, disease, and defeat by becoming a man of faith. His name was Jabez, and most men in his position would have given up and resigned themselves to the position that nothing could be done about their situation.

If you have been tempted to believe that there is no hope for you to become a man of faith, I invite you to come into the light of God's Word and discover that by daring to believe the promises of God you can revolutionize your life.

It worked for Jabez, and it will work for you as well.

WHAT'S IN A NAME?

"Now Jabez was more honorable than his brothers, and his mother called his name Jabez, saying, 'Because I bore him in pain.' And Jabez called on the God of Israel saying, 'Oh, that You would bless me indeed, and enlarge my territory, that Your hand would be with me, and that You would keep me from evil, that I may not cause pain!' So God granted him what he requested" (1 Chronicles 4:9–10).

Do you recognize the miracle in the brief account of the man Jabez? It may be a bit obscure until you realize that his name, *Jabez*, means "sorrow, pain, and trouble." His name tells of the condition of his life, and now that is understood, you'll see that he chose to change his destiny.

Names in the Bible have significant meaning, and in many instances they are meant to communicate a message. A person's name in the Bible often conveyed the type of person he or she would become, or what he or she was to do for God.

For instance, the name *Jacob* means "deceiver," and he became just that. Deception defined Jacob's life. When God met with Jacob and changed his life, He also changed his name to fit his new life. His new name was *Israel*, meaning "a prince" (Genesis 32:28).

Abram meant "high father," but God changed his name to fit his destiny. He called him *Abraham*, which means "father of many nations" (Genesis 17:5).

Moses' name told of his life, as it means "draws out" (Exodus 2:10). Every time his name was spoken, it reminded Moses that his life had been preserved when Pharaoh's daughter drew him out of the water as a baby.

Joshua means "savior." On a daily basis, Joshua was reminded by his name that he was a savior of his people. This is precisely what he became as he led Israel into the Promised Land.

It was the same with Jabez. His mother bore him in sorrow. How so? Was he crippled or afflicted with some weakness or disease from birth? Was he simply born in an atmosphere of sorrow, trouble, and heartache? Whatever the case, every time his name was called, it cried out to him, "You are pain! Trouble! Sorrow!"

In my imagination, I picture Jabez as a young man becoming convinced that his destiny would always be confined and limited to weakness, sickness, and pain, for his very name spelled it out. Who can tell the negative effects of that message in his mind and spirit? There must have been a constant struggle before he gave in to the lie that there was no hope for him.

FAITH AND THE WORD OF GOD

Faith comes by hearing the Word of God (Romans 10:17), and in my mind's eye I see the day when Jabez heard a prophet of God proclaim the unlimited power of the God of Israel. I can almost hear the prophet declare how God delivered the children of Israel from Egypt with signs and miracles.

He tells of God's manifest presence in the wilderness through the pillar of fire by night and the cloud by day (Exodus 13)!

He tells of God's miracle manna and miracle meat in the desert (Exodus 16)!

He tells of God's miracle water that came forth out of the rock (Exodus 17)!

He tells of miracle shoes and clothes that did not wear out through forty years of wandering the desert (Deuteronomy 29:5)!

He tells how God miraculously healed two million sick, weak, and downtrodden slaves as they came out of Egypt. "And there was none feeble among His tribes" (Psalm 105:37).

Then I hear the prophet cry out with Jeremiah, "Ah, Lord GOD! Behold, You have made the heavens and the earth by Your great power and outstretched arm. There is *nothing too hard for You*" (Jeremiah 32:17).

I hear this man declare the promise of God: "Call to Me, and I will answer you, and show you *great and mighty things*, which you do not know" (Jeremiah 33:3).

I can imagine that when Jabez heard these words of faith, hope began to rise up within him. He realized that *with God all things are possible.*

WHEN FAITH RISES

When Jabez saw God's truth, he rebelled against the devil's lie!

When he saw God's light, he rebelled against the darkness!

When he saw God's life, he rebelled against disease and death!

When he saw God's liberty, he rebelled against bondage!

The faith of Jabez began to rise and caused him to cry out to God. He became angry at his so-called destiny. He rebelled against the unbelief and doubts, and he became a man of faith!

He turned his eyes to the… great Jehovah God who had declared, "I am the LORD who heals you."

"And Jabez called on the God of Israel saying, 'Oh, that You would bless me indeed, and *enlarge my territory*, that Your hand would be with me, and that You would keep me from evil, that I may not cause pain!' *So God granted him what he requested*" (1 Chronicles 4:10).

Jabez wanted God to bless him, but he wanted more. He wanted to be loosed and freed. "Enlarge my territory!" he cried.

"Deliver me from the confining walls of fear, disease, defeat, and pain! Enlarge my territory! Raise me up from this life of pain! Open these doors! Break down these iron gates! *Enlarge my territory!*"

He also asked something very important in his prayer. He prayed that God would keep him from evil. He was saying, in effect, that he wanted to be healed and delivered in order to serve the living God. He would not use his freedom from fear, sickness, and trouble to serve Satan. Jabez wanted to live a life pleasing to God.

The Bible says, "God granted him what he requested." Jabez was free! He would not believe it was his destiny to go through life with pain and sorrow. He turned his eyes away from his name to *the name of the great Jehovah God* who had declared, "I am the LORD who heals you" (Exodus 15:26).

JABEZ CHANGED HIS DESTINY, AND SO CAN YOU!

You can change the whole course of your life by looking at the promises of God and daring to believe them. Jesus said, "And you shall know the truth, and the truth shall make you free" (John 8:32).

The first step to freedom and healing and miracles is to come to grips with God's truth in the Bible.

A woman who had been very sick told me one day

how she was finally healed by the miracle-working power of God. She said, "Pastor Osteen, *I read the promises of God over and over and over until I suddenly saw that God wanted to heal me.*" When she believed that God really wanted to heal her, it was easy to have faith. Today, she is perfectly healthy.

God does not want you sick or to suffer in pain. Your trouble and sorrow did not come from your loving heavenly Father. God is Jehovah-Rapha, "the LORD your healer" (Exodus 15:26).

Jesus said, "The thief does not come except to steal, and to kill, and to destroy. I have come that they may have life, and that they may have it more abundantly" (John 10:10). It is the devil who tries to steal your health, kill your hopes with discouragement, and destroy your life.

Jesus came that you might have life and have it more abundantly. This is your hour to enjoy abundant life. The will of God is that you might be victorious in the trials of life and not suffer defeat!

Jesus came all the way from heaven to bring you deliverance. When He came, He came for *you*. When He died, He died for *you*.

"Surely He has borne our griefs (sicknesses, weaknesses, and distresses) and carried our sorrows and pains . . . and with the stripes [that wounded] Him we are healed and made whole" (Isaiah 53:4–5 AMP).

"Himself took our infirmities and bore our sicknesses" (Matthew 8:17). "Who heals all your diseases" (Psalm 103:3).

Just as Jesus bore your sins, He bore your sicknesses. It is not God's will for you to bear your sins, and it is not His will for you to bear your sicknesses.

"For this purpose the Son of God was manifested, that He might destroy the works of the devil" (1 John 3:8). "Resist the devil and he will flee from you" (James 4:7).

Rise up in faith! Refuse to live a life of defeat!

Take these promises and climb up into the presence of God! Change your destiny by calling upon the God of miracles!

God is speaking to you now: "If you ask anything in My name, I will do it" (John 14:14). "And my God shall supply all your need according to His riches in glory by Christ Jesus" (Philippians 4:19).

I have seen multitudes change their destinies by believing these promises and refusing to give in to the enemy.

Men of Faith Rise Up and Fight

You must see that it is Satan who wants you to suffer. It is God who wants you to be blessed. Do not passively accept sickness, sorrow, trouble, or circumstances as

I read the promises of God over and over and over until I suddenly saw that God wanted to heal me.

your destiny in life. Choose to believe what God's Word says about you.

Resist the devil and he will flee from you! Unless you do, you cannot be delivered. Put your trust and faith in God and His mighty Word.

Years ago, a man came to our church a broken man. He was a single father of four children, had lived a life of poverty and hurt, and was barely making it financially. When he put his faith in Christ, he began to give his tithe to the Lord and pray that God would bless him financially. I was impressed that he brought his children to church faithfully and even volunteered his time. I was aware that he worked hard in the medical field but was low on the totem pole. He gave his best and worked with excellence. The doctors took notice of his excellence and faithfulness and began to ask for his assistance. God gave him such favor with the doctors that he decided to start his own business and began to sell the medical equipment to these doctors. God blessed his business, and today he is a successful businessman. Later, he met a wonderful Christian lady, and he and his whole family are serving God together because this man chose to believe that God had a better life for him. *He changed his destiny!*

The Lord Jesus is with you as you read these promises of His power and willingness to deliver you. Begin to praise Him right now for your healing and victory. Praise Him even though you may feel discouraged or sick.

As Jabez did, pour your heart out to God. Press in to touch the hem of His garment. Do not be stopped or discouraged. God wants you to have *abundant life*.

Faith comes by hearing the Word of God, and as you act upon it, the miracle-working power of God is released. The word of the apostles to the crippled man in Acts 3 was, *"In the name of Jesus Christ of Nazareth, rise up and walk"* (Acts 3:6). As a result, the man rose up and went walking, leaping, and praising God into the temple! You, too, can be set free from sickness, addictions, anger, sin, and depression in Jesus' Name!

As was true of Jabez, you can become a man of unwavering faith! Begin to do what you could not do before! Put action to your faith! Give God the glory and know that God is about to enlarge your territory!

Reflections from
JOEL

*M*y *father grew up with a "poverty mentality," and for years in the ministry, he thought he was doing God a favor by staying poor. God tried to bless and increase my dad, but he couldn't receive it. Later, Daddy learned that as God's children, we are able to live an abundant life; that we should even expect to be blessed as was Jabez. Indeed, it is as important to learn how to receive a blessing as it is to be willing to give one.*

Friend, don't sit back and allow negative, critical thoughts to influence your life. The Bible tells us to be "transformed by the renewing of your mind" (Romans 12:2). When you dwell on God's Word and start seeing the best in situations, little by little, one thought at a time, you will transform your thinking. God will help you. Stay full of faith. Stay full of joy. Stay full of hope. God will transform your life!

CHAPTER TWO

A Man *of* Faith Believes *the* Word *of* God

I once visited the Vatican in Rome. There are numerous paintings and statues of the twelve apostles on the walls and in the halls, and they're all bigger than life. In fact, some of them are huge. I think it's safe to say that the artists and sculptors captured the way we tend to think of the apostles—towering men of faith who rose up and changed the world.

But the apostles weren't bigger than life—they were flesh and blood just like you and me. Somehow, because they're in the Bible, we think they weren't like us. But that's not true. They were ordinary men, with wives and children and bills and all of life's challenges.

In the book of 1 Kings 17 and 18, the Old Testament prophet Elijah was a man of great faith, one whom I admire deeply, but the apostle James tells that he also "was a man with a nature like ours" (James 5:17; 1 Kings 17:1).

Nature means "passions and sufferings." He was an ordinary man just like you and me, subject to the same passions we have.

Yet Elijah had such great faith that *when he prayed that it wouldn't rain, it didn't . . . for three and half years!* "And he prayed earnestly that it would not rain; and it did not rain on the land for three years and six months. And he prayed again, and the heaven gave rain, and the earth produced its fruit" (James 5:17–18; 1 Kings 18:42–45).

You're probably thinking, *Pastor Osteen, how can a person have enough faith to stop the rain—period? Let alone for three and half years.*

To answer that, let's start where the Word of God starts. The Bible says, "But without faith it is impossible to please Him, for he who comes to God must believe that He is, and that He is a rewarder of those who diligently seek Him" (Hebrews 11:6). It also states that without faith in God, it's impossible to be born again or to go to heaven: "For by grace you have been saved through faith, and that not of yourselves; *it is the gift of God*, not of works, lest anyone should boast" (Ephesians 2:8–9).

So that we all have the same capacity to receive the gift of salvation, God has given each of us the same measure of faith. The apostle Paul wrote, *"God has dealt to each one a measure of faith"* (Romans 12:3). God wants every

Know what the Word says, take it to God in faith, and believe He will cause it to come to pass in your life.

person to come to saving faith, and we all start out with the same measure, the same size of faith—enough capacity to bring us to salvation.

Once we accept Jesus Christ as our Savior and Lord, through our salvation we "become the righteousness of God in Him" (2 Corinthians 5:21), and we can never be more righteous than that. We cannot grow in righteousness.

But we can and must grow in faith. Clearly, the Bible says, "Your faith is growing more and more" (2 Thessalonians 1:3 NIV). To become a man of unwavering faith requires that you grow mightily in your faith as Elijah did in his life.

How Faith Grows

The more you use your arms and legs, the more you walk and jog and exercise, the stronger and fitter your muscles become. But if you don't use a muscle, you'll lose it.

That's the way faith is. Faith will

grow as you use it. The more you use it, the stronger it grows. But this growth is a gradual process.

You aren't disappointed in a baby because he can't stand or run a marathon. You don't expect a baby to do that, but you do expect the child to grow, become stronger, start crawling, then pull himself up and hold on to things, and finally to take a step or two. Eventually, you know the child will be able to walk and run.

That's the way your faith is. It grows gradually as you use it. Many people make the mistake of trying to jump up and run in their faith life when they are just babies learning to crawl.

I asked a man one time, "What do you do?" He said, "I don't work. I just live by faith." It was no surprise to me that he was deep in debt. That kind of behavior is not faith; it's ignorance. The Bible says if any man doesn't work, he shouldn't eat (2 Thessalonians 3:10).

I remember when my congregation and I began to believe God for our first new buildings. Our first sanctuary had been converted from a feed store and seated 234 people. In 1969, I had been having great evangelistic meetings all across the country, and things had gone well. During my absence, we needed to expand, so a new church was built to seat 700 on adjacent property.

After I returned to Lakewood Church, it was clear

that more expansion was in our future, but I realized my faith for getting new church buildings wasn't very strong. I had not really exercised my faith in that area, and my faith had not been truly challenged. The first thing God showed me was to gather a group of men from the church. He showed me what each man was able to do and how to challenge each man to have faith to do what he could toward one building and then another.

We developed a little bit . . . then a little more. In 1975, a wing was added on each side of the auditorium to seat a total of 1,800. In 1977, the building was again expanded to seat 4,000 and then to 5,000 seats in 1979. Then, we stretched our faith muscles and a beautiful 120,000-square-foot sanctuary seating 8,200 was dedicated debt free in 1988. In 1991, we dedicated a two-story, 37,000-square-foot Children's Center, where we ministered to over 2,500 children weekly. Then a Family Life Center, a three-story, 62,000-square-foot office and educational building, was completed debt free in 1993. We started small and worked toward the big.

You need to develop your faith gradually as you go along. Use your faith. Stretch your faith, or it will never grow.

Faith Is Believing the Word of God

Faith is simply believing God will do what He said

He will do. It is believing the Word of God. The New Testament uses two Greek words for the Word of God. One is *logos*, which is the revealed will of God, the plan of salvation, contained in the Bible. The other is *rhema*, which is a word God speaks to you personally. Suddenly, a scripture comes alive because God Himself is speaking it to you directly.

Faith not only comes from the *logos*; faith comes by hearing the *rhema* of God (Romans 10:17). Once God illuminates, speaks, or brings His Word to your attention, believing it is easy, because with that *rhema* comes faith.

There have been many times when God has quickened particular scriptures to me as I was reading, and it was as if He were reading it straight to me. He made a promise in His Word, I read that promise, and then He quickened that promise to me. I knew the promise would come true, because I had both the *logos* (the written Word) and the *rhema* (the spoken Word). My faith was strong, because I knew God would do what He said He would do.

Elijah Acted on the Word of God

Elijah understood this. He didn't just decide one day, "Well, I'm a man of faith, and I'm tired of rain, so I'm going to stand out here and stop the rain. It's a slow day, and I don't have much to do. I haven't seen many miracles lately, so I'll just call on God to shut up the heavens."

No, when Elijah prayed, he was functioning in the *logos*, the Word of God, and I believe God quickened it to his heart. How so? Imagine that one day Elijah was reading the covenant between God and Israel in Deuteronomy 11:13–17, and the Lord quickened it to him.

This passage states, "So if you faithfully obey the commands I am giving you today—to love the LORD your God and to serve him with all your heart and with all your soul—then *I will send rain on your land in its season, both autumn and spring rains, so that you may gather in your grain, new wine and oil.* I will provide grass in the fields for your cattle, and you will eat and be satisfied. Be careful, or you will be enticed to turn away and worship other gods and bow down to them. Then the LORD's anger will burn against you, and *he will shut the heavens so that it will not rain and the ground will yield no produce,* and you will soon perish from the good land the LORD is giving you" (NIV).

Elijah knew the Word of God and was painfully aware that the people had turned away from God to worshipping the idol Baal, a false god. Clearly, God promised He wouldn't send the rain if the people turned to false gods. So when he prayed that God would shut up the heavens, he was praying in the knowledge of God's

Word. Elijah held God's Word up to Him and prayed earnestly for God to keep His Word, and He did.

A man of faith knows what the Bible says. When you're going through a trial, find what God says in the Bible and hold it up to Him. Remind Him of what He said. "Put Me in remembrance; let us contend together; state your case, that you may be acquitted" (Isaiah 43:26).

You perhaps are asking, "Well, if God says He's going to do it, why doesn't He just do it? Why do I have to remind Him?" Because *prayer is the power that moves the hands of God*. And when you stand on God's Word and remind God of His promise, it makes your faith grow. It strengthens your trust in God.

For example, God isn't automatically going to bring your children to faith. Deuteronomy 28:41 states that one of the penalties for sinning is that you'll have children but not enjoy them. Now, as a Christian, Christ has redeemed you from the curse of the law (Galatians 3:13). You can stand before God and say, "God, You said if I served You, I would enjoy my children. I believe You are going to fulfill Your promise because You never lie." And God will begin to act in your behalf to bring that promise to pass.

God isn't automatically going to fill your bank account with money. The curse of the law is to want things but to be poor and to drag through life. The Bible says that

Faith is simply believing God

will do what He said

HE WILL DO.

Christ redeemed us from that curse. God's blessing is that you will be the head and not the tail, you will lend and not borrow, you will be on top and never on the bottom (Deuteronomy 28:12–13).

As Elijah did, you must know what the Word says, take it to God in faith, and believe He will cause it to come to pass in your life.

Elijah Had a Showdown on the Mountain

God clearly stated that He would stop the rain, so why didn't He do it before? He was waiting for someone who would read the covenant, act on it, stand on it, and believe Him to bring the results. Elijah had to believe and act on that promise from God, which he did, and for three years and six months it didn't rain.

Then Elijah had a remarkable showdown with the 450 prophets of Baal before the children of Israel on Mount Carmel. He told the people, "Get two bulls for us. Let them choose one for themselves, and let them cut it into pieces and put it on the wood but not set fire to it. I will prepare the other bull and put it on the wood but not set fire to it. Then you call on the name of your god, and I will call on the name of the LORD. The god who answers by fire—he is God" (1 Kings 18:23–24 NIV).

The prophets of Baal spent all day trying to call down

fire from heaven. They cut themselves and went through all their ceremonial rigmarole. Elijah stood over to the side and taunted them. "Shout louder," he told them. "Maybe your god is asleep or on a trip." Finally, the exhausted prophets gave up.

Then Elijah gathered the people around. He repaired the altar of the Lord with twelve stones and dug a trench around it. He arranged the wood, cut the bull into pieces, and laid it on the wood. Then he told the people to fill four large jars with water and pour it on the altar. The people filled the water jugs and poured them on the offering three times. Elijah wanted to be sure nobody thought there was any trickery involved.

Then Elijah prayed, "O Lord, God of Abraham, Isaac and Israel, let it be known today that you are God in Israel and that I am your servant and have done all these things at your command. Answer me, O Lord, answer me, so these people will know that you, O Lord, are God, and that you are turning their hearts back again" (1 Kings 18:36–37 niv). And fire fell from heaven, burning up the sacrifice, the wood, and even the stones, the soil, and the water in the trench around the altar.

The people responded by falling down and crying, "The Lord—He is God!" Then Elijah commanded them to seize the 450 prophets of Baal and kill them, which they did in obedience.

Given what had happened, Elijah then went off by himself to pray for rain. Why?

Because the people had repented and turned back to God. Now, according to Deuteronomy 11:13–17, they were in a position to receive rain, but the rain wouldn't automatically come. Elijah had to earnestly pray for rain. He had to stand in faith and believe that God would honor His Word just as He did when the rains stopped.

That is what you have to do to get your needs met. Even though God has promised it, and you see that it belongs to you, you're going to have to earnestly pray in faith, believing God will do what He said.

You can't just sit around and say, "Well, God said He would do it, and I'm going to just let Him do it." No, life is a fight. The apostle Paul said to fight the good fight of faith (1 Timothy 6:12). You have to take hold of your victory.

You have to rise up and earnestly pray, even though God has already said it. There has to be some effort on your part. You have to exercise your faith and believe God for the answer.

That's what Elijah did. He was a man of faith, and in the next seven chapters I will show you how Elijah demonstrates seven qualities of a man of unwavering faith.

Reflection from
JOEL

Growing up, my family had a big German shepherd named Scooter, and he was king of the neighborhood. Scooter was strong and fast and looked like he could fight a tiger. But one day a spunky Chihuahua raced out of a house toward Scooter, barking up a storm. The closer that little dog got, the more Scooter hung his head like a coward. When the Chihuahua finally got face-to-face with Scooter, Scooter just lay down, rolled over, and put all four legs up in the air.

Even though we know that we have all God's resources at our disposal, we do something similar when adversity barks. Often, we roll over and say, "I quit. This is too tough." Instead, it's time to tap into God's power, stand up, and fight.

CHAPTER THREE

A Man *of* Faith Sees *and* Hears What *the* World Cannot See *and* Hear

As demonstrated on Mount Carmel by the prophet Elijah, the first quality of a man of unwavering faith is that he will see and hear what the world cannot see and hear.

After the 450 prophets of Baal had been killed, Elijah found the wicked King Ahab and announced to him, "Go, eat and drink, for there is the sound of a heavy rain" (1 Kings 18:41 NIV). At that moment there wasn't any sign of rain in the sky, but *Elijah knew God would keep His Word*.

Remember, God had said, "If you break My law and worship idols, I'll keep the rain from you." Elijah had taken that word and prayed, and God had shut up the heavens. Then Elijah had seen the people repent from their idolatry, and based upon God's promise, Elijah knew he had the right to call upon God for the rain to return.

Elijah's spirit began to reach out. He knew what God was going to do. He said, "This is how faith works. I don't see the rain. I don't smell it or hear it. But I tell you, in my spirit, I hear the sound of abundance of rain."

How faith works reminds me of a dog whistle. If you blow a dog whistle, you won't hear a sound. But if there's a dog nearby, his ears will perk up. He can hear that whistle, because he hears on a different sound frequency than we do.

In the same manner, people attuned to the Holy Spirit can hear on a different frequency than the world. We can hear things the world does not hear. We can hear the sound of angels' wings, the sound of the footsteps of Jesus, and the coming blessings of God.

Men and women of faith hear the shout of victory before it ever gets there. They can hear the sound of that wayward son or daughter coming home. By faith, they can hear them knocking on the door. They can hear the testimony of that loved one for whom they've been praying for years. They hear it with the ears of faith.

How did Elijah hear the rain that no one else could see or hear? *Because he knew the Word of God.*

What No Eye Has Seen or Heard

Several years ago a friend of mine was flying in a jet at

35,000 feet on his way to a preaching appointment. At the time, he was such an accomplished pianist that he had been offered opportunities in the entertainment world that would have assured him a great future. He also had a beautiful solo voice. God had called him to preach, and he had chosen to follow the vocation that was the perfect will of God for his life.

Several years before this flight, he had been afflicted with rheumatoid arthritis, which had grown progressively worse in his entire body. His hands became knotted and gnarled and paralyzed to free movement, ending his days of artistry at the piano. All the joints of his body were affected by this disease and filled with pain. His ankles were swollen to the size of grapefruits, and his knees were enlarged.

My friend was unable to function in a normal way. He told me he bought aspirin by the full box rather than the bottle. He took it constantly to try to relieve the excruciating pain that was throughout his body. Many mornings he had to be rolled out of bed with the help of others and placed in a tub of hot water to loosen up the joints and partially relieve the pain. He was not able to walk in a normal fashion, but simply made his way along the best he could with his knees and ankles and the rest of his joints aching and deformed by this crippling disease.

This was his condition as he sat on the airplane

going to preach the Gospel. The doctors had given him the verdict that there was nothing that medical science could do for him as far as there being any permanent healing. He could only get relief from the pain by taking medication. They told him that he would just simply have to live with it and gradually grow worse.

Gone was his ability to thrill and bless people with piano music. Gone was his ability to live a normal life. But he sat on that airplane, determined to preach the Gospel to the best of his ability.

While reading his Bible on the airplane, he began to meditate on the Scriptures. He read that Jesus bore our sicknesses and carried our pains and by His stripes we are healed (Isaiah 53:5). He read in Matthew 8:17 that Jesus healed all the sick: "That it might be fulfilled which was spoken by Isaiah the prophet, saying: 'He Himself took our infirmities and bore our sicknesses.'" He read in 1 Peter 2:24, "Who Himself bore our sins in His own body on the tree, that we, having died to sins, might live for righteousness—by whose stripes you were healed."

Suddenly, a light turned on deep inside of him. He heard in his inner man the words, "By His stripes *you were healed.*" There came a true understanding on the inside of him. Suddenly, he knew that he was healed! Suddenly, he had absolute assurance that he was free

If you hear the word impossible ringing in your ears, then listen to the sweet voice of the Son of God.

from that disease. He began to rejoice, because he was certain he was healed.

As he sat in his seat with this revelation knowledge that he was healed, he didn't look any different; his body didn't feel any different; his body didn't function any different. No one seated around him could see the miracle. But he knew that a miracle had taken place on the inside.

When he went to deplane, he could barely make it out of his seat, then he hobbled down the aisle. The pastor from the church met him at the airport gate, took his little case, and asked, "How are you?" And my hobbling friend, still stooped over and unable to look up in a normal fashion, turned his head slightly (as far as he could) to look upward toward the pastor and said, "Oh, I'm glad to announce to you that I'm healed by the stripes of Jesus."

I'm sure the pastor wondered if not only his body had been affected by the disease, but maybe his mind also!

When the time came for my friend to minister at the pastor's church, he hobbled to the platform and stood behind the pulpit. With the arthritis seemingly still dominating his body, he looked up at the congregation and said, "Before I preach the message to you, I would like to rejoice before all of you and tell you that I am so glad that by the stripes of Jesus I have been healed. Arthritis cannot live in my body. I want you to rejoice with me that I am healed and that I can play the piano and walk normally again."

Every person in that congregation reacted in a different way. I am sure many of them wondered about the credibility of the man standing stooped in the pulpit.

But from that moment on, my friend began to get better and better. In a matter of weeks, all the arthritis was gone from his body and every joint was normal. That was well over twenty years previous to this writing. I have been in his meetings personally and wept as he played the piano and gave praise to the Lord Jesus Christ. Truly he is living a healthy life to this day!

Faith Is of the Heart

So what happened on the airplane to my friend? What happened to Elijah on Mount Carmel? Is there a law that supersedes the natural laws that we know? Is there something that we don't know as far as our natural minds are concerned?

The Bible talks about the law of faith, stating that "the law of the Spirit of life in Christ Jesus has made me free from the law of sin and death" (Romans 8:2). You see, sitting on that airplane, my friend received knowledge from God in his spirit-man that the world is unable to receive with the natural, carnal mind.

The Bible says that faith is of the heart. "For with the heart one believes . . ." (Romans 10:10). It is with your heart that you believe. The *heart* means "the spirit-man." There is a spirit-man on the inside of your physical body. The apostle Paul is telling us that faith is a spiritual force that comes forth from the spirit-man. It is the spirit-man who is able to respond to the Word of God and to exercise faith.

You see, as my friend sat on the airplane, filled with a crippling disease that had held him captive, he meditated on the great promises of the Word of God concerning the eternal redemption that we have in the Lord Jesus Christ. He meditated on it until suddenly it was not only in his carnal mind, but his spirit-man began to pick up these truths. His inner man began to feed upon the truths of God's Spirit.

It was Spirit-to-spirit communication. When his spirit began to pick up the eternal fact that "by His stripes you were healed," faith leaped into being, because faith is of the heart. He suddenly knew, not with his mind, but with his spirit-man, that he was healed. In this *knowing*, he was unwavering in his confidence, even though there was no physical evidence of a change.

You see, the body has five senses—sight, hearing, taste, smell, and touch—with which we contact the physical world. But God has given us a sixth sense—faith—to function in the spirit realm in our spirit-man, made alive with the life of Almighty God. Yes! The spirit-man made alive by the grace and resurrection life of Jesus Christ does have a sense, which we call faith. Faith is totally independent of the five senses we use to function in the physical and material world.

This sense of faith is used to touch the unseen, invisible world. The natural senses cannot touch that spiritual dimension. They have no contact with it. But faith, created by the Word of God, enables you to reach out into the dimension of the invisible and activate the creative power of God.

This is what happened to my friend on the airplane: He left the natural and went into the supernatural. He left the physical and went into the spiritual. He got out of his physical nature and got into his spiritual nature. Feeding on the Word of God, his spirit-man received revelation knowledge and an unshakable confidence that he was truly healed. Though there was no evidence anywhere in his physical senses to corroborate the fact that he was healed, this sixth sense of faith dominated and conquered the others! His body responded, and sickness and disease left him.

That is what it means to become a man of unwavering faith. Are you there? Do you realize there is hope? It is possible for you to rise out of your prison house, whatever that might entail for you!

Jesus said, "With men this is impossible, but with God all things are possible" (Matthew 19:26). Jesus said this to enlarge our faith to believe God for what we think or perceive to be impossible.

As you look at your situation today, is it impossible with men? Is it impossible for you to be healed or for your family to be put back together or for that situation to be resolved or that addiction to end? If you hear the word *impossible* ringing in your ears, then listen to the sweet voice of the Son of God who cannot lie: "With men this is impossible, but with God all things are possible" (Matthew 19:26).

By faith you can shake off the shackles that hold you

in the natural and touch God who is in the realm of the supernatural. Study the truths presented in this book until you too can rise above the word *impossible.* Begin to function in the realm of unwavering faith.

Elijah heard the rain that

no one else could hear

because he knew the Word of God.

Reflection from
JOEL

*P*erhaps as you're reading my father's words you're saying, "I don't want to get my hopes up. I've prayed. I've done everything I know to do. Nothing's changed. If I don't get my hopes up and nothing good happens to me, at least I won't be disappointed."

Friend, you must get your hopes up, or you won't have faith (Hebrews 11:1). Consider the captivating account of two blind men who heard that Jesus was passing by. When Jesus heard their cries for mercy, He posed an intriguing question: "Do you believe that I am able to do this?" (Matthew 9:28). Jesus wanted to know whether they had genuine faith. The blind men answered, "Yes, Lord; we believe." Then the Bible says, "[Jesus] touched their eyes and said, 'Become what you believe'" (v. 29 THE MESSAGE). What a powerful statement about their faith! You will become what you believe!

CHAPTER FOUR

A Man *of* Faith Prays Earnestly Even Though He Has Heard *the* Answer

The Bible says that after the prophet Elijah announced to King Ahab that rain was coming and the king went off to eat and drink, "Elijah climbed to the top of Carmel, bent down to the ground and put his face between his knees" (1 Kings 18:42 NIV).

So if *by faith* Elijah heard the sound of abundance of rain (v. 41), why didn't he just put his mantle over his head, walk home, and call it a good day? Couldn't he have said, "I heard the rain; it's coming. There's no need for me to stay around here"? No, Elijah knew it was time to go before God in earnest prayer, or prevailing prayer, to be sure that what he had heard by faith would come to pass.

Hearing the answer you need by faith doesn't mean you don't have to pray and to claim your victory. It doesn't mean there isn't a battle to go through. We must "fight the good fight of faith" until we "lay hold on eternal life, to which [we] were also called" (1 Timothy 6:12).

When my wife, Dodie, was diagnosed with metastatic cancer of the liver in 1981 and was given only a few weeks to live, we got on our faces in our bedroom and we prayed in faith, agreeing with God's Word that "by the stripes of Jesus [she] was healed." Even though we knew the truth of God's will as revealed in His Word, we had to return again and again to God's promise and keep holding onto that Word in faith believing for many, many months, until healing was manifest in her body.

As demonstrated on Mount Carmel by Elijah, the second quality of a man of faith is that he prays earnestly in faith even though he has already heard the answer.

PREVAILING PRAYER AND THE MAN OF FAITH

Prayer is our contact and conversation with God, and it is a significant key to becoming a man of faith. The fact is that our very lives should be a constant prayer. The apostle Paul admonishes us to "Pray without ceasing" (1 Thessalonians 5:17). We can and should talk to God at any time, day or night, whether we are on our knees or not. It's not the position of our bodies that God is interested in as much as the condition of our hearts. We can talk to God no matter where we are or what we're doing. And whether our prayers are verbal or in thought, they can be equally effective.

Prayer can be in the form of praise, fellowship, declaring the Word, or even resisting the enemy. But most important, *prayer must prevail over circumstances*. That was true for the prophet Elijah, and it is true for any man of faith today.

Prevailing prayer is frequent, continuing, effective, and persuasive. We must learn how to have a prevailing prayer life. The Bible is specific about the things that are necessary, if we are to be successful in the life of prevailing prayer.

Pray With a Sense of Righteousness

"Confess to one another therefore your faults (your slips, your false steps, your offenses, your sins) and pray [also] for one another, that you may be healed and restored [to a spiritual tone of mind and heart]. The earnest (heartfelt, continued) prayer of a righteous man makes tremendous power available [dynamic in its working]" (James 5:16 AMP).

James indicates that the continued prayer of a righteous person, a man of faith, creates tremendous power. And that power is available *when we pray scripturally*—not necessarily just because we pray, but because we pray according to God's Word, as Elijah demonstrated.

The prayer that really prevails before God is the prayer that honors the great redemptive truth of the New Covenant—that we are new creatures in Jesus Christ. Because of our relationship with Jesus, the Righteous One, we are righteous, and we have the right to come boldly to the throne of grace in order to obtain mercy and grace in time of need (Hebrews 4:16).

Prevailing prayer comes from the calm, sensible acceptance of the fact that we are the righteousness of God, not from arrogance or pride. Prayer that is based on your right to be in the presence of God makes tremendous power available—to meet your needs and walk in victory in your personal life.

Delight Yourself in the Lord

"Delight yourself also in the Lord, and He will give you the desires and secret petitions of your heart" (Psalm 37:4 AMP). This is another way to have prevailing prayer in your life—*delight yourself in the Lord.*

You cannot pay any attention to folks who try to discourage you. There are always those who criticize God's people and discourage faith. When David was dancing with joy before the Lord (2 Samuel 6), he was dancing so high that his skirts were coming up and showing his legs. His wife Michal was watching from a window and

REGARDLESS OF YOUR

circumstances,

rejoice in the Lord.

despised him in her heart. When David came in all happy and glowing with faith, she said to him, "How glorious was the king of Israel today, uncovering himself today in the eyes of the maids of his servants, as one of the base fellows shamelessly uncovers himself!" (2 Samuel 6:20).

David's response to Michal was to continue to delight in the Lord: "It was before the LORD, who chose me instead of your father and all his house, to appoint me ruler over the people of the LORD, over Israel. Therefore I will play music before the LORD. And I will be even more undignified than this, and will be humble in my own sight" (vv. 21–22).

Regardless of your circumstances, rejoice in the Lord. Habakkuk 3:17–18 states, "Though the fig tree does not blossom and there is no fruit on the vines, [though] the product of the olive fails and the fields yield no food, though the flock is cut off from the fold and there are no cattle in the stalls, yet I will rejoice in the Lord; I will exult in the [victorious] God of my salvation!" (AMP).

Be happy when you talk with the Lord—enjoy your time with Him. Delight yourself in His presence. No matter what happens, men of faith should be glad in the Lord. God wants us to prosper. But even if we owed money to everybody in the world and had all kinds of trouble, we still have Jesus Christ and eternal life! We are going to heaven, where there is no sighing or dying, no pain or sorrow, and it will last forever!

ASK IN THE NAME OF JESUS

Jesus says to us, "I assure you, most solemnly I tell you, if anyone steadfastly believes in Me, he will himself be able to do the things that I do; and he will do even greater things than these, because I go to the Father. And I will do [I Myself will grant] whatever you ask in My Name [as presenting all that I AM], so that the Father may be glorified and extolled in (through) the Son. [Yes] I will grant [I Myself will do for you] whatever you shall ask in My Name" (John 14:12–14 AMP).

Jesus went to the Father, and He is our representative there. Fellowship with Jesus, talk with Jesus, and pray in His Name as a man whose faith is anchored in Him alone.

Now consider what Jesus told His disciples right after He explained to them that He was going to die. He said, "So for the present you are also in sorrow (in distress and depressed); but I will see you again and [then] your hearts will rejoice, and no one can take from you your joy (gladness, delight). And when that time comes, you will ask nothing of Me [you will need to ask Me no questions]. I assure you, most solemnly I tell you, that My Father will grant you whatever you ask in My Name . . .

Up to this time you have not asked a [single] thing in My Name . . . but now ask and keep on asking and you will receive, so that your joy (gladness, delight) may be full and complete" (John 16:22–24 AMP).

God wants you to come to Him in faith and ask in Jesus' Name that your joy may be full and complete.

Pray in Faith Without Wavering

Jesus died and rose again. He went to the Father so that we might have the privilege of prevailing prayer as men of faith. And we are instructed to ask in faith, with no wavering.

"If any of you is deficient in wisdom, let him ask of the giving God [Who gives] to everyone liberally and ungrudgingly, without reproaching or faultfinding, and it will be given him. Only it must be in faith that he asks with no wavering (no hesitating, no doubting). For the one who wavers (hesitates, doubts) is like the billowing surge out at sea that is blown hither and thither and tossed by the wind. For truly, let not such a person imagine that he will receive anything [he asks for] from the Lord, [for being as he is] a man of two minds (hesitating, dubious, irresolute), [he is] unstable and unreliable and uncertain about everything [he thinks, feels, decides]" (James 1:5–8 AMP).

God does not want our faith to be based on our

present conditions. We should not be tossed about by the circumstances of life. God wants us to believe His promises and hold to them without wavering. He wants our faith to remain constant.

We don't have to beg God for what He has already promised us in His Word. We are to exercise our faith and enter into His presence with confidence. We just ask and accept—without any doubt. We can say, "Father, I found this promise in Your Word, and I thank You for it!" This should make going to the Father a real joy. Be happy and rejoice—that's part of our prayer and praise to God.

Pray With the Right Motives

Be careful when you pray that you don't ask with the wrong motives and for the wrong purpose. We must ask for the right reasons.

"What leads to strife (discord and feuds) and how do conflicts (quarrels and fightings) originate among you? Do they not arise from your sensual desires that are ever warring in your bodily members? You are jealous and covet [what others have] and your desires go unfulfilled; [so] you become murderers. [To hate is to murder as far as your hearts are concerned.] You burn with envy and anger and are not able to obtain [the gratification, the contentment, and the happiness that you seek], so you fight and war. You do not have, because you do not ask. [Or] you do ask [God for them] and yet fail to receive, because you ask with wrong purpose and evil, selfish motives. Your intention is [when you get what you desire] to spend it in sensual pleasures" (James 4:1–3 AMP).

In order to have prevailing prayer in our lives, we must be sure to not ask for our own selfish purposes. For instance, some people pray to be healed with no intention of living for God. Some pray for financial help without intending to honor God with their tithe. This is praying with selfish motives and dishonoring God. "The heart is deceitful above all things, and desperately wicked: who can know it?" (Jeremiah 17:9). When we pray, we must approach God with a sincere and humble heart.

In order to prevail in prayer, we must make sure our motives are right. We need to be tied into the great purposes of God.

ASK IN LINE WITH THE WILL OF GOD

The will of God is the Word of God. If we are not asking for something that is in God's Word, our prayers are useless. But if we are asking in line with God's will, we have His promise that He will answer us. "And this is the confidence (the assurance, the privilege of boldness) which we have in Him: [we are sure] that if we ask anything (make

Prayer that is based on your right to be in the presence of God makes tremendous power available.

any request) according to His will (in agreement with His own plan), He listens to and hears us" (1 John 5:14 AMP).

There are many, many promises in God's Word, and we have a right to enjoy them all. Salvation, healing, prosperity, a happy marriage and family, and salvation for our loved ones are in His Word. We can ask all of these things in confidence, knowing that God will listen to us and hear us, because they are promised in His Word.

"And if (since) we [positively] know that He listens to us in whatever we ask, we also know [with settled and absolute knowledge] that we have [granted us as our present possessions] the requests made of Him" (1 John 5:15 AMP). In other words, we know that if God said it, we've got it! We don't have to beg God for the things He has promised us.

So we can pray with confidence, no matter the need, knowing God will hear and answer our prayer as long as we are praying in accordance with His Word.

Pray With a Clear Conscience

"Whenever our hearts in [tormenting] self-accusation make us feel guilty and condemn us. [For we are in God's hands.] For He is above and greater than our consciences (our hearts), and He knows (perceives and understands) everything [nothing is hidden from Him]" (1 John 3:20 AMP).

Sometimes Christians try to justify the wrong things they are doing, and they have a battle going on down inside themselves. Perhaps they have allowed some things in their lives that shouldn't be there. But that sin produces an aggravation in the believer's life. Because we are born of God and have His nature, we can't habitually practice sin and enjoy it (1 John 3:9). We can never love it.

The apostle John continues, "And, beloved, if our consciences (our hearts) do not accuse us [if they do not make us feel guilty and condemn us], we have confidence (complete assurance and boldness) before God, and we receive from Him whatever we ask, because we [watchfully] obey His orders [observe His suggestions and injunctions, follow His plan for us] and [habitually] practice what is pleasing to Him" (1 John 3:21–22 AMP). Here the beloved John clearly spells out four specific things that we should be doing in order to receive from God.

First, *watchfully obey His orders*. God delights in answering the prayers of those who are always interested in obeying Him. The Scriptures are full of ways we are to be obeying the Father as men of faith, whether it is walking in holiness, loving our wives and children, being the spiritual leader in our home, or ruling our families so as to guard them from the evil one. That is one of the things we must do in order to have prevailing prayer in our lives.

Second, *observe His suggestions*. Most Christians strive to obey God's orders, but as our relationship with Him grows, God has enough confidence in us that He sometimes makes suggestions and lets us make up our own minds. It is a wonderful thing to be so in tune with God that we respond to His slightest suggestion: "My son, I wouldn't do that" or "That's not My best for you." The hearts of His children beat to please Him, and He knows that He can trust them.

Third, *follow His plan*. As a man of faith, the most important thing in the world is to get into God's plan for your life. God is the architect of the universe. If He can put together a universe as intricate as ours and see to every meticulous detail, surely He can draw a plan for our lives. There is a good, acceptable, and perfect will of God for you (Romans 12:2). And in order to experience the power of prevailing prayer, we must follow God's plan for our lives.

Fourth, *habitually practice what is pleasing to God.* Make it a point to find out what is pleasing to God and make living that way a priority in your everyday life. Listen to what the Bible says about how we are to live: "Do not love the world or the things in the world. If anyone loves the world, the love of the Father is not in him. For all that is in the world—the lust of the flesh, the lust of the eyes, and the pride of life—is not of the Father but is of the world. And the world is passing away, and the lust of it; but he who does the will of God abides forever" (1 John 2:15–17).

As you follow these simple guidelines, you can learn many ways to enjoy and practice prevailing prayer in your life. As a man of unwavering faith, make prayer a constant and enjoyable part of your life.

Reflection from
JOEL

When I was growing up, a man attended our church whose hands were so crippled with arthritis, he could hardly use them. But one day he heard my father preaching about forgiveness, and how the lack of forgiveness keeps God's power from operating in our lives and prevents our prayers from being answered. He began asking God to help him get rid of anger and resentment in his heart toward those people who had hurt him over the years. As he forgave, the most amazing thing began to happen. One by one, his fingers straightened, and eventually, God restored his hands to normal.

You may see your prayers answered more quickly as you let go of the past and rid yourself of bitterness and resentment.

CHAPTER FIVE

A Man *of* Faith Is Strong When There Is No Evidence *of the* Answer

In the account we have been following of the prophet Elijah and his servant on Mount Carmel, he told his servant, "'Go and look toward the sea….' And he went up and looked. 'There is nothing there,' he said" (1 Kings 18:43 NIV).

As demonstrated by Elijah, the third quality of a man of unwavering faith is that his faith is strong when there is no evidence of the answer. Men of faith keep going even when they don't see the answer coming. When the situation says, "There's no evidence that God is going to answer," you go on because you have the Word of God.

Elijah kept believing when he saw nothing happening in the physical realm. That's precisely what God started with in the beginning. He created the universe out of nothing. So if you want to be God-like, start with nothing and speak the Word of God until what you desire comes into being. He is the God who "calls those things which do not exist as though they did" (Romans 4:17).

Maybe you have nothing. You've just about given up. You've prayed, you've looked to God, and there's still nothing to show for it. People are telling you, "It's not working!" *Stand your ground. Keep holding the Word of God up to Him.*

In Jeremiah 1:12, the Lord says, "I am watching to see that my word is fulfilled" (NIV). *If God promised it, He will do it.*

Lord, Open Our Eyes!

Elijah knew, and a man of faith knows, that life is a battleground. But he also comes to understand that the battle is won when he listens to his spirit-man rejoicing over what he *knows* to be true by faith through revelation knowledge gained through the Word of God.

In 2 Kings 6, an amazing story is told of the prophet Elisha, who was the disciple of Elijah. The Syrians were fighting the Israelites, and every time the Syrians moved, the Israelites knew where their enemies were ahead of time. So the Syrian leader got all the people together and said, "I want to know something in this counsel of war. Who is for Israel, and who is for us? There must be a spy in the camp."

One of the servants responded, "None, my lord, O king; but Elisha, the prophet who is in Israel, tells the king of Israel the words that you speak in your bedroom" (v. 12). They said, "You mean there is a prophet down there who can understand these things?" Yes was the response, so they sent the whole army out to get that one man! That is how afraid the enemy was of the man of God. They sent an army down to get Elisha.

That is the way it is going to be with us. God is going to move in the supernatural. You may not know it, but the enemy is afraid of you. The Bible states, "Therefore submit to God. Resist the devil and he will flee from you" (James 4:7). Satan trembles at the very thought of you as a man of faith.

The servant of Elisha awoke in the morning and looked out at the great host of the Syrian army, with its chariots and horses. All this young man could see was the enemy, and his natural response was to panic and cry out, "Alas, my master! What shall we do?" (v. 15).

But when Elisha got up and walked out to assess the situation, he also saw those hundreds and possibly thousands of Syrian horses and chariots out there and said, "Do not fear, for those who are with us are more than those who are with them" (v. 16).

I can imagine that young man saying, "Elisha, I don't

know how you're counting, but one plus one equals two, and we are clearly outnumbered!"

Elisha responded, "'LORD, I pray, open his eyes that he may see.' Then the LORD opened the eyes of the young man, and he saw. And behold, the mountain was full of horses and chariots of fire all around Elisha" (v. 17). The host of heaven surrounded the Syrians!

Elisha didn't say, "Look, God just created some angels." No, those angels were there in the invisible world all the time. Just because God manifested their presence by making them visible in the physical dimension at that moment did not change the fact that they were already present. The answer was there all the time.

Walk Into the Forest of God's Eternal Truths

What was true for the servant of Elisha is true for us as we begin to experience God's touch upon our lives. You see, salvation has existed for you ever since Jesus died and purchased it with His blood. Healing has been yours, eternal life has been yours, and financial blessing has been yours.

Sometimes you do not immediately see your new job or your healing or prosperity or your victory over an addiction, but that does not mean it is not yours. Just as your angel is by your side and you are convinced by

Walk out into the Word of God— the great forest of God's eternal truths— and you will find the abundance of God.

the Word of God that he lives in that invisible world watching after you, so too your healing or your prosperity is there. As far as God is concerned, His promises are all yours. You can rejoice by faith that they are yours, even though they have not yet been manifested.

Suppose I told my wife, "Dodie, I put one thousand dollars in your coat pocket for you to spend on whatever you want. It is in the coat hanging in the hall closet." Think of what she would do. First, she would rejoice because she believes me. Second, she would begin to make plans as to how she would use it. Third, she would begin talking to everyone around about the blessing and joy she had received.

Even though she does all these three things, she has not yet seen or felt or heard the rustle of the thousand dollars. All she has is the word of a person she loves and trusts. But because she believes me, she talks, rejoices, and makes plans by faith that I am true to my word.

Isn't it strange how we will act on the word of a lawyer, a doctor, a financial planner, or a loved one, and yet won't act on the Word of God? A man can lie, but God cannot lie!

As you walk out into the Word of God—the great forest of God's eternal truths—you will find the abundance God has put in your pocket as a man of faith. He freely gives you salvation, healing, prosperity, strength, victory, and the ability to overcome temptation and Satan. It is all there in the spirit world. It is in your spiritual pocket. You have not yet touched it. You have not seen or felt it yet. All you have is the Word of Almighty God who cannot lie!

By faith you can reach into the invisible area and experience God's power at work in your life.

Consider this truth: "Now faith is the assurance (the confirmation, the title deed) of the things [we] hope for, being the proof of things [we] do not see and the conviction of their reality [faith perceiving as real fact what is not revealed to the senses]" (Hebrews 11:1 AMP).

Faith goes into the Word of God, believes God, and foresees as real fact what is not yet revealed to the five physical senses. "By faith we understand that the worlds [during the successive ages] were framed (fashioned, put in order, and equipped for their intended purpose) by the word of God" (Hebrews 11:3 AMP). The worlds were equipped and fashioned by the Word of God.

Isn't it silly that some people never venture into the treasure house of God's eternal truths and then wonder why they don't have any faith or any ability to believe God? Oh, how this truth ought to make us live in the Word of God!

God Is!

As a man of faith, you must start with the Word of God and believe that the invisible *God is*. "But without faith it is impossible to please Him, for he who comes to God must believe that He is, and that He is a rewarder of those who diligently seek Him" (Hebrews 11:6). *The invisible God is!*

Not only is God there, but every blessing we need is there, and the first principle is to believe that they *are,* without seeing any evidence. Did Jesus die for your healing? Prosperity? Salvation? Blessings? Victory over sin and the powers of darkness? Yes, yes, yes, yes, yes.

You must believe that this invisible God is a rewarder of those who diligently seek Him, and that you must diligently seek His invisible blessings. The Bible says that we should read the Word of God and seek Him as for hidden treasure, as for gold and silver (Proverbs 2:4). If you will diligently seek any blessing you find in the Word of God, God will reward you by manifesting it to you.

When the blessing or promise manifests, the man of faith isn't shocked. Instead, he says, "I knew what happened today was already mine all the time. I've been praising God continually, because I saw it was done in that invisible world, and now it's visible!"

Do you need a confirmation of that truth? "By faith Noah, being divinely warned of things not yet seen, moved with godly fear, prepared an ark for the saving of his household, by which he condemned the world and became heir of the righteousness which is according to faith" (Hebrews 11:7). Noah was informed by God of an event of which there was *no visible sign as yet*.

You see, as men of faith, that's all that happens to us. We step into God's bank filled with His magnificent eternal truths, and God says, "Here are My promises for you. I have them in your name, so receive them by faith."

The Building Blocks of Faith

The Old Testament character Gideon was threshing wheat behind a winepress, hiding for fear of the enemies of Israel. He was frustrated, fearful, discouraged, and feeling like a failure. God sent an angel to him, but the angel didn't say to him, "Hail, thou scaredy cat. Hail, thou cringing coward!"

The angel came to Gideon from the invisible world and said, "The LORD is with you, you mighty man of valor!" (Judges 6:12).

Gideon responded, "Who else is here? Do you mean to tell me that I am a mighty man of valor?"

Now, the angel could have and might well have said, "Yes, that is exactly how God sees you. It's all yours, whether you ever take it or not. You are a mighty man of valor. I bring you news from the spirit world!"

Gideon rose up and began to act as though he were a mighty man of valor, and he found out he was! His story of bringing deliverance to his nation is legendary.

This is the exact principle that Jesus Christ was teaching in Mark 11:24: "Therefore I say to you, whatever things you ask when you pray, believe that you receive them, and you will have them." Jesus asks you to believe it is yours in the invisible realm on the basis of God's Word. He does not ask you to believe that it is already manifested in the physical realm. But He said that as you believe it in the invisible realm, He will see that you get it in the visible, physical realm.

As a man of faith, *believe you receive in the faith realm, and you shall have it in the natural realm.*

God is a Creator. He wants you to join hands with Him to see His miraculous power create things for your every need. He wants to help you reach the world with the good news about Jesus. The building blocks for God's creative power are not in the natural realm, but the invisible.

Our business as men of unwavering faith is to believe that what God says is true, to confess it, to rejoice about it, and to act as though it is true. Jesus will see that it is manifested. These are the building blocks of faith.

STAND YOUR GROUND.

Keep holding the Word of God up to Him.

Reflection from
JOEL

It's interesting to note the difference between the way Gideon saw himself and the way God rewarded him. Although Gideon felt unqualified, full of fear, and lacking in confidence, God addressed him as a mighty man of fearless courage. Gideon felt weak; God saw him as strong and competent to lead His people into battle and victory. And Gideon did!

Moreover, God sees you as a champion. He believes in you and regards you as a strong, courageous, successful, overcoming person. You may feel unqualified, insecure, weak, fearful, and insignificant, but God sees you as a victor! What you feel doesn't change God's image of you. God still sees you exactly as His Word describes you. Learn to see yourself as your heavenly Father sees you. He loves you and has destined you to win in life.

CHAPTER SIX

A Man *of* Faith Never Gives Up!

At the beginning of the previous chapter, the prophet Elijah was praying on Mount Carmel and had sent his servant to look toward the sea for rain clouds. The servant climbed up the hill and looked out toward the sea, then gazed and gazed as far as the eye could see. When he went back, he told Elijah, "There is nothing there."

Elijah responded, "Go look again."

So the servant went a second time and looked. He came back and said, "There's still nothing there."

Elijah told him, "Go look again."

The servant went a third time, a fourth time, a fifth time, and a sixth time. I imagine he got pretty tired. Every time his answer to Elijah was the same. "There is nothing there." Each time Elijah prayed a little bit more, then told him, "Go look again."

"Seven times he [Elijah] said, 'Go back'" (1 Kings 18:43 NIV).

Elijah kept on praying. He kept on believing and resting in faith. He had seen God's promise in the Word. He had already heard the sound of rain in his spirit. Elijah knew if God said it, He would do it. So he just kept sending his servant to look again.

As demonstrated by Elijah, the fourth quality of a man of unwavering faith is that he keeps going back to God's promise and expecting Him to fulfill it.

When you get discouraged and it looks as though God isn't sending the answer, go again to the Word of God. Read it again. Remind God again of His promise. Go two times, three times, four times—however many times it takes—until the answer comes! Keep going back. Don't give up.

Faith Is Not an Emotion

To become a man of unwavering faith, you need to get it settled in your heart that *faith has nothing to do with emotion—nothing.* Faith is simply acting on the Word of God, believing He told you the truth. Some people wait for some great manifestation of faith. They expect goose bumps or lightning bolts! That is ridiculous! Faith is an act!

Faith is not an emotion. *Faith is believing and acting on a legal contract based on God's Word.*

This truth can change your life. When you read a scripture that you can apply to your life, faith grows in your heart. You can simply receive God's Word and begin to act as though it is so, as Elijah did.

I want all of the Word of God to profit me. Even though the Word was preached to the Israelites in the wilderness, it did not profit them, because it was not mixed with faith. Hebrews 4:3 says, "For we who have believed do enter that rest . . ." When you believe, you enter into rest! You don't have to wring your hands in worry and fear.

Those who believe enter into God's rest. "There remains therefore a rest for the people of God. For he who has entered His rest has himself also ceased from his works as God did from His" (Hebrews 4:9–10).

Faith Has a Divine Rest

Faith rests. *When God's Word gets down into your heart and you know that God has heard you, there is an unshakable rest.* Your part is to seek God and study His Word every day. Meditate on His truths until one day a sweet, divine rest engulfs you. Then you will know that everything is all right. Faith has rest. No matter how much the storm blows and the wind howls around you, you can have rest.

Years ago there was a painting contest. Each painting was to illustrate peace and rest. There were many entries—beautiful paintings of pastoral scenes, majestic mountains, seascapes, and sunsets.

But right in the midst of these tranquil scenes was a painting of a storm. Storm clouds hung low on the horizon, and the lightning was flashing across the black sky with such detail that you could almost hear the thunder. There were mountains in this picture, and right in the crag of a rock, hiding from the wind, was a little mother bird with her nest safe in the cleft of a rock. She sat there singing with all her might while her little brood was in the nest. This is a picture of real peace and rest.

That little bird had known by instinct that all the winds of this world could not blow that mountain down! The same Creator who created safety for the bird is your heavenly Father, who will keep you safe throughout all the storms that life can bring. The divine rest that God gives is not necessarily getting to a place where you don't have any storms. Jesus' rest can be yours in the midst of the storm!

As we have seen in Elijah's example, from the time you read and believe the Word of God and the time that you actually see the manifestation of the answer, you can rest, knowing that God is faithful to His Word.

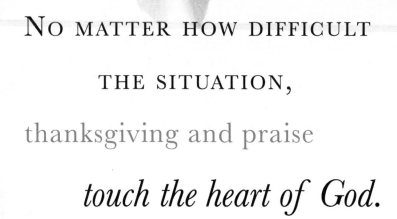

No matter how difficult
the situation,
thanksgiving and praise
touch the heart of God.

A LIFE OF FAITH AND PRAISE

As you wait in faith for the finances to arrive, for a child to come home, for emotional stability and the overcoming of fear, or whatever you are desiring from God, *what shows your unshakable confidence in God is a life of praise for God and His Word alone.* You can enjoy rest that simply looks up into the face of God and praises Him, because you know God loves you and is true to His Word.

The Bible states, "Those who sacrifice thank offerings honor me, and to the blameless I will show my salvation" (Psalm 50:23 NIV).

When you believe that God has given you the desire of your heart, but there is as yet absolutely no outward manifestation, you should live a life of praise that glorifies God and confesses the Word in joy before the Father's throne.

I have three daughters, who are always wanting new dresses. Suppose my little girl comes and says to me, "Daddy, I want a new dress. Please!" I would say to her, "Darling, this is Monday, but if you will trust me and wait a bit, I will buy you that dress on Saturday." Similar to my previous illustration of the thousand dollars in my wife's coat, my daughter would leap for joy, because she knows she is going to get that dress on Saturday. She trusts that I will deliver what I've promised, so between Monday and Saturday all she does is live in joy. She'll tell everyone she meets about the new dress.

Notice that I only spoke to her once about the dress. She never came back to make sure I wasn't lying to her. She knows that my word is good from Monday until Saturday, and she knows that Saturday is coming.

Years ago, when I was writing the book *There's a Miracle in Your Mouth*, I was in the greatest pain of any time in all of my life. I had muscle spasms in my back, and I couldn't sleep at night. I had such excruciating pain in my back, it seemed as though every disc were ruptured and every vertebrae were out of place.

During those weeks of writing, I was tormented with thoughts such as, *You're going to have to have surgery, and you'll end up paralyzed, in a wheelchair, and never live a normal life again. You are a hypocrite. While you sit there writing your miracle book, you are sicker than anybody! You are not going to get well. There's no miracle in your mouth or life. Why should you tell anybody else about how to get well? It's not working for you.* Those were haunting lies and the chiding of Satan!

Despite the pain and sleepless nights, I would get up in the morning, go outside, and walk and talk to God.

I would say, "Father, I praise and thank You that I have received my healing. Galatians 3:13 says, 'Christ has redeemed us from the curse of the law, having become a curse for us (for it is written, "Cursed is everyone who hangs on a tree").' Thank You that I did receive my healing at the very moment I asked You. I have received it. I know this is Monday, but *I thank You that Saturday is coming.* I am going to spend from now till Saturday just praising You. Yes, I praise and thank You, Father."

As I praised God and thanked Him for the manifestation of the answer, I could see myself out of that situation. I could see myself delivered. I became filled with joy as I beheld myself completely healed!

Praising and thanking God when you are in the midst of a battle gives the enemy a nervous breakdown! It puts him on tranquilizers! As I prayed on Monday, I looked forward to Saturday. I knew that God had promised me more than a new suit. I knew that healing was mine. I did not spend my time begging or questioning God, but with an unshakable confidence in the Lord, I just praised Him.

After I finished writing *There's a Miracle in Your Mouth,* the pain left me, and I have never had a bit of back trouble since that time! The Bible teaches us to live a life of praise.

Praise Is Faith at Work

When you say what God says about your situation, you will begin to see yourself as God sees you. You can allow trials to shake your confidence in God or you can trust God. Doubt and fear come when you believe the circumstances rather than God.

God says of Abraham: "He did not waver at the promise of God through unbelief, but was strengthened in faith, giving glory to God" (Romans 4:20). He grew strong in faith, giving praise to God. You see, he praised God before he ever saw Isaac. *Sarah did not conceive Isaac until she was ninety years old and Abraham was ninety-nine—twenty-four years after God had spoken the promise.* Yet Abraham just looked up to heaven and said, "Saturday's coming! Saturday's coming!" He praised God and grew strong in faith as he looked at the Word of God and praised God that His Word is truth! He had an unwavering confidence in God.

In Joshua 6, we read the story of Joshua marching around the walls of the city of Jericho. They went around praising God and shouted *before* the walls fell down.

Praise is faith at work. Between Monday and Saturday we should praise God, because the answer is on the way!

In 2 Chronicles 20:21–22, King Jehoshaphat heard

that a vast army of Moabites and Ammonites had come against Judah to battle. King Jehoshaphat was so overwhelmed by the news, he began to seek the Lord, proclaimed a fast, called the people together to seek the Lord and ask for His help. He reminded God of His promise to hear them when they cried to Him in a time of affliction and He would hear and save them. As a result, the Spirit of the Lord came upon the prophet Jahaziel who proclaimed, "The Lord says to you: Be not afraid or dismayed at this great multitude; for the battle is not yours, but God's." Based upon that Word from God, the king sent singers out before the army, saying, "Praise the Lord; for His mercy endures forever," and the opposing armies turned on each other and destroyed one another! The battle was won miraculously because they began to praise the Lord! *Praise was their secret weapon.*

Perhaps you say, "Jesus certainly would not have to praise God before a manifestation of a promise of God." If you think that, you need to read the story of Jesus raising his friend Lazarus from the dead (John 11). In that situation, when Jesus came to Bethany, they told Him all about Lazarus' death. "Therefore, when Jesus saw her weeping, and the Jews who came with her weeping, He groaned in the spirit and was troubled. And He said, 'Where have you laid him?' They said to Him,

Faith is not an emotion. Faith is believing and acting on a legal contract based on God's Word.

'Lord, come and see.' Jesus wept" (John 11:33–35).

Jesus was so merciful and compassionate. The Jews mocked Him, thinking wrongly that He wept for sorrow and despair. Some of them said, "Could not this Man, who opened the eyes of the blind, also have kept this man should from dying?" (v. 37). Jesus gave a groan in Himself. He came to the grave, which was a cave with a stone in front of it. He told them to take away the stone, even though Lazarus had been dead for four days.

In verse 40, Jesus said, "Did I not say to you that if you would believe you would see the glory of God?" They then took away the stone, and Jesus lifted His eyes and said, "Father, I thank You that You have [past tense] heard Me." Lazarus was still dead, but Jesus was saying, "Father, I thank You that he is alive. I thank You that he is out of the grave." Jesus praised God *before* Lazarus was raised from the dead.

Actually, Jesus was saying, "Father, I thank You that You have heard Me. I have already received the answer to My prayer. I already see Lazarus raised. I thank You that You *have* heard Me." Jesus praised the Father when there was no evidence of life. It is not that you are *going* to be victorious; you *are* victorious.

You must be able to stand in the midst of all the evidence of deadness and say, "Father, I thank You that You have heard me. I am healed. I am delivered. I have the desires of my heart."

Between Monday and Saturday, we will praise God and rest in Him. Praise is faith at work!

Offer a Sacrifice of Thanksgiving and Praise

Consider the story of Jonah: "Now the word of the LORD came to Jonah the son of Amittai, saying, 'Arise, go to Nineveh, that great city, and cry out against it; for their wickedness has come up before Me.' But Jonah arose to flee to Tarshish from the presence of the LORD" (Jonah 1:1–3). Instead of obeying God, Jonah ran the other way.

Have you ever run away from God? Jonah didn't get far, and neither will you. If you read his story, you know that Jonah ended up being thrown overboard and swallowed by a great fish. He found himself on the inside of that fish, in the slime and gastric juices and with seaweed wrapped around his head. I'm sure he was certain he would die.

Yet, in the midst of all that, Jonah found deliverance. "Then Jonah prayed to the LORD his God from the fish's belly" (Jonah 2:1). Did you know that you can pray in a fish's belly? If he could pray inside of a fish, you can certainly pray in the midst of your trouble!

Jonah prayed to the Lord out of the fish's belly: "I cried out to the LORD because of my affliction, and He answered me. Out of the belly of Sheol I cried, and You heard my voice. For You cast me into the deep, into the heart of the seas, and the floods surrounded me; all Your billows and Your waves passed over me. Then I said, 'I have been cast out of Your sight; yet I will look again toward Your holy temple.' The waters surrounded me, even to my soul; the deep closed around me; weeds were wrapped around my head. I went down to the moorings of the mountains; the earth with its bars closed behind me forever; yet You have brought up my life from the pit, O LORD, my God" (Jonah 2:2–6).

Notice that Jonah then recalled, "When my soul fainted within me, I remembered the LORD" (Jonah 2:7). If you can just get your eyes on the Eternal, Almighty God who created heaven and earth, there is hope for you.

Remember God when your son has gone astray or

your daughter has fallen by the wayside. Remember God when your business has failed. Remember God when the doctor says you can't live. Remember God when the situation looks dark. Jonah said, "I remembered the Lord."

Then consider Jonah 2:9. "But I will sacrifice to You with the voice of thanksgiving." What did Jonah do between Monday and Saturday while sitting in that fish? He offered the sacrifice of thanksgiving and praise.

Are you sitting in the belly of a fish today? Does it feel as though Saturday will never come? Are you to cry, beg, and doubt God? Or are you to sit there and say, "Mr. Fish, you may look like you've swallowed me forever, but I have remembered the Eternal God. I have His Word. Salvation is of the Lord. I know that He will get me out of this situation. I see myself out of it. I will offer the Lord the sacrifice of thanksgiving and praise. I praise You, Lord, that I am coming out of this terrible situation."

No matter how difficult the situation, thanksgiving and praise touch the heart of God. All God has to do is speak to your fish, and the fish will instantly spit you out. In Jonah's case, he came out on dry ground, running and preaching!

If Jonah could praise God in the midst of a fish, can't you praise God in the midst of a physical discomfort?

Can't you praise God in spite of seeing fish every place? Can you look up into the face of God and just praise Him with joy because you already see your child serving God, your home filled with peace and love, and the situation in your business already resolved?

Praise is the secret to a man of faith developing an unwavering confidence in God.

Resistance to Your Faith Will Surely Come

Know that the enemy will try to shake your confidence in God. Let me share an incident from my own life that illustrates this truth.

We used to have a convention every year during Thanksgiving at Lakewood Church, during which we would serve food to the people. One year I determined that I was going to pray that God would give us money to buy two head of cattle or that someone would give us two head of cattle to feed all the visiting missionaries. I stood before our congregation and asked them to pray with me.

But Saturday didn't come soon enough. I waited and waited as the convention neared, but there were no cattle, not even a cow. One day I began to think, *You're not going to get those cows. You have the money in the bank to buy those cows, so there's no use of worrying over this.*

I shook myself and said, "I believe God has supplied

us some cattle." But the truth was that I was getting weaker and weaker.

A few days later I heard a voice saying to me, "Why go through all of this? You have the money, and you're busy preaching and teaching. You don't have time to mess with trying to have faith for two cows. Just buy them."

That made sense to me. So I became quiet about it, and I decided to just go buy the meat, and no one would ever care. I can remember the very minute I let go of believing God for the cows. Something left me out of my spirit. I released it. I gave up and lost my confidence. I didn't lose confidence in a doctrine or a scripture, but in a Person.

I bought the meat, we had a great convention, and I thought I got away with it. However, a few days later the Lord gave me a visitation in a dream in the night. In this visitation, He took me down a lonely country road where I saw the biggest snakes I have ever seen in my life. They looked forty to fifty feet long. The Lord had me walk up close to the snakes and gaze at them. As I got closer, I noticed that two of them were bulging with a distinct outline of a cow—the head, shoulders, backbone, and hipbone. There was a cow in both snakes. Then the Lord said to me, "I just want you to know that you let the devil swallow your cows!"

I learned a valuable lesson from this experience. This

principle of faith in God will give you the same joy on Monday or Friday as you will have on Saturday! Why? Because God's answer is yours the very moment you pray and believe you receive it. It is yours, and you can rest in that fact!

Every day you should praise God for what He has promised you. If you have a physical need, even if the symptoms rage in your body, do not put your attention on the symptoms. When Peter was walking on the water, his eyes were fixed on Jesus (Matthew 14:29–30). Did you know that the waves were just as high and the wind was just as strong when he was walking as it was when he sank? He walked because he did not look at the waves; he looked at Jesus. But when he turned his attention to the waves and wind, he sank.

Jesus is the Word of God. He is the Living Word. No matter how high the waves billow or how strong the wind may blow, do not get your attention on them. Just keep on walking toward Jesus!

Every contrary thing that comes against you financially, mentally, emotionally, morally, maritally, physically, or any contrary thing that tries to get you to doubt God's Word, should be the very indication to you that you need to keep on looking at Jesus. Keep your eyes on the Word of God.

REMEMBER: SATURDAY IS COMING!

How would you act today if you had what you are believing for? What if you actually saw and touched the manifestation? How happy would you get?

This is how you should feel and act right now! As you praise God, fear and anxiety will fall away from your life. It may be on a Monday that your heavenly Father says that He will supply all your needs and give you the desires of your heart. It may not yet be Saturday, but Saturday's coming. All you need to do is spend your time praising the Lord. Settle it in your heart as to what your specific desire is. Then picture yourself having it, release your faith, and start praising God.

When you praise God and rejoice and rest in His presence, disease departs, demons flee, and the enemy is defeated. Don't think it is a burden to do this, but know that this is faith at work!

This is how you begin exercising your faith by your praise and your words of praise. Saturday will come!

Reflection from
JOEL

Life is all about how you choose to see things. You can complain about your boss, or you can thank God for your job. You can complain about mowing the lawn, or you can thank God that you have a yard. You can complain about the price of gas, or you can thank God that you have a vehicle.

Years ago, I was driving in a pouring rainstorm. I lost control of my car and spun out on the freeway, crashing into the guardrail and almost getting run over by a huge eighteen-wheeler. Amazingly, I came out of that crash without a scratch, but my car was wrecked. A friend thought I'd be upset about my car, but I was just grateful to be alive. I made up my mind to let God's praise continually be in my mouth (Psalm 34:1).

CHAPTER SEVEN

A Man *of* Faith Goes On When There's Just *a* Little Evidence

After the prophet Elijah's servant had made six trips to the top of the mountain to look for a cloud, "The seventh time the servant reported, 'A cloud as small as a man's hand is rising from the sea'" (1 Kings 18:44 NIV). The servant gazed out over the sea and saw a tiny cloud, not very promising, but he ran back to tell Elijah.

As demonstrated by Elijah, the fifth quality of a man of unwavering faith is he continues to believe and expect the victory when there is just a little evidence. The whole answer hasn't come yet. The need hasn't been completely met. But he keeps on believing.

You say, "I'm believing for my healing. I've been hurting all over, and I have a little relief. But it's so little." Or, "I'm believing for a financial need. I did get one bill paid, but I have a hundred more. It's so little."

Faith goes on when there's just a little cloud in the sky—not a big thunderhead, but a little white cloud no bigger than a man's hand.

There were many times when my wife, Dodie, was fighting her battle with cancer that she saw nothing. In 1981, she was diagnosed as having metastatic cancer of the liver with only a few weeks to live. The doctors said there was nothing they could do, but she knew what God has promised in His Word. She held it up to Him and reminded Him that by His stripes she was healed (1 Peter 2:24). She continued to pray and believe for her complete healing even when her body was in pain and there was no evidence she would be healed.

There were many times when she had to say, "Go again. Go again. Look once more." And then she got a little relief—just a little. So she made a list of all the symptoms she was believing would leave her body. She kept speaking the Word of God in the face of the symptoms and began to check them off, one by one. She saw very little at first, but she went on. And today, she is completely healed!

Dodie's remarkable story of healing is told in her book *Healed of Cancer*. If you see nothing, if you see just a little, go on, as she did. Hang in there. Pray earnestly. Put God in remembrance. Don't give up, and don't let Satan steal what belongs to you.

Come to Jesus

I love the story of Jesus and the leper in Matthew 8:1–3. "When He had come down from the mountain, great multitudes followed Him. And behold, a leper came and worshiped Him, saying, 'Lord, if You are willing, You can make me clean.' Then Jesus put out His hand and touched him, saying, 'I am willing; be cleansed.' Immediately his leprosy was cleansed."

I am convinced that Jesus did not love that leper any more than He loves you or me. He is the *very same Jesus today* as He was the day this leper was healed. Most of us who read this want what he received from Jesus, but we will not receive it because we only *think* we have done what he did.

As men of faith, this is the great lesson we learn from the leper: *He came to Jesus.*

The leper recognized that *Jesus is the Healer*. You cannot have healing without the Healer; the benefit without the Benefactor; the blessing without the Blesser. You cannot separate the gift from the Giver! Only God can heal, and the secret is to come to Jesus. He is full of compassion and mercy. He bore your sins and sicknesses on the cross (Matthew 8:17).

Do not bar the door of your heart against Jesus. Let Him in.

If you send for a doctor and let him in the front door of your house, but refuse to let him into the bedroom where the patient is, he can do very little good. Our hearts have many rooms. Some are locked and barred with bad memories, unconfessed sin, bitterness, and other things. Open wide every door to Jesus. *He cannot do you any good until you let Him go where the trouble is.*

In my own life, I received Jesus as my Savior, trained for the ministry, and had preached for many years, yet I had a serious condition in my stomach—ulcers. Why was I not healed? I had received Jesus into the front door of my heart, but there were many rooms barred to Him.

I believed the days of healing and miracles were over.

I did not know if I believed in demons or not, but I was certain it was beneath my dignity as a preacher to be caught casting out demons.

It embarrassed me to be around people who were always lifting their hands and praising the Lord. And I felt that those who spoke in tongues were emotional people who lacked a little in mentality!

Later, when I was baptized with the Holy Spirit and spoke in tongues, I unlocked every door and opened them wide so Jesus would have free access to *all my heart*, and He came in His fullness. Whenever the Healer comes, there is healing. I don't remember when I was healed, but I suddenly discovered I no longer had ulcers! Years have passed, and I am still healed.

The leper did more than just come to Jesus. *He came humbly to Jesus.* He came beseeching Him, worshiping Him, and falling on his face before Him. I humbled myself and fell before the Lord. I lifted my hands and heart in adoration and praise to His holy Name, and healing came. "Let everything that has breath praise the Lord. Praise the Lord" (Psalm 150:6).

Settle All Doubts About the Will of God

The leper allowed Jesus to *settle all doubts* about the will of God.

I can well imagine this man meeting with several other lepers. They talk about this wonderful man Jesus. One says, "But it is not God's will to heal people like us. We are suffering for God's glory. We are being chastened." Another says, "How could this be the will of God? This seems more like the will of *hate* than the will of *love*." Turning to the man who came to Jesus, I imagine they ask him, "What do you think?" He replies, "I don't know, but I think it is His will. I hope it is His will. I think I'll go ask Him and find out."

When he gets to Jesus, he says, "Lord, if You will (if it is Your will), You can heal me."

Jesus didn't take long to settle the matter. He said, "I will!" This is the only man who asked about the will of God concerning healing, and Jesus settled it: *It is His will to heal you!*

When our first daughter was born, she had signs of brain damage. Based on her symptoms—no sucking reflexes, no muscle tone, difficulty swallowing, couldn't lift her arms or legs or head—the doctors said Lisa had something similar to cerebral palsy. We could see clearly with our eyes she had something seriously wrong with her. I had, up to this time, taken the typical attitude of Christians about healing. I would pray, "If it is your will . . ." I can never remember very much ever happening as a result of that prayer. But now we had to find out what the will of God was.

I wanted to know what Jesus would do for *my baby!* I wanted to know the will of God.

If I wanted what the leper got, I had to do what he did. I had to settle the matter of the will of God.

So I closed myself in my library. It was filled with books telling me how miracles had passed away. I didn't want arguments *against* the willingness of God to heal. I

Open wide every door to Jesus. He cannot do you any good until you let Him go where the trouble is.

wanted all the help I could get. I set my face toward God, determined to find the truth from His Word. Praise the Lord, I found it!

I discovered sickness was not from God. Satan is the one who comes to steal, kill, and destroy.

When God made Adam and Eve, He made them without blind eyes, deaf ears, and diseased organs. If He had wanted and willed these things, He would have made Adam and Eve that way.

It was Satan who caused Job's sickness. "So Satan went out from the presence of the LORD, and struck Job with painful boils from the sole of his foot to the crown of his head" (Job 2:7).

Jesus said that Satan had bound the woman with a spirit of infirmity, and she was bent over and could not straighten up into a normal standing position (Luke 13:11–16).

In Matthew 12:22, the Bible states that this man's blindness was caused by the devil.

In Mark 9:17–27, we read the record of a boy who had convulsions and who was deaf and dumb. Jesus said it was all caused by a foul spirit and cast it out.

Jesus healed many people during His earthly ministry. The Bible tells us all these people were oppressed of the devil. Satan was the cause of their sickness. "How God anointed Jesus of Nazareth with the Holy Spirit and with power, who went about doing good and healing all who were *oppressed by the devil*, for God was with Him" (Acts 10:38).

This settled one thing in my mind. God had not afflicted our baby. This trouble came from Satan. It was not something to be coddled as a gift from God. It was something to be refused and fought against.

You will never rebuke your sickness as long as you think God sent it. You must know that *God wants you well!*

Who Heals All Your Diseases

The triune God is a *Trinity of Healing*. God is a Healer. "I am the Lord who heals you" (Exodus 15:26). He does not change. "For I am the Lord, I do not change" (Malachi 3:6).

The Lord Jesus is a Healer. The four Gospels record His mighty deeds, and Hebrews 13:8 says that He is the same yesterday, today, and forever.

The Holy Spirit is a Healer. "But if the Spirit of Him who raised Jesus from the dead dwells in you, He who raised Christ from the dead will also give life to your mortal bodies through His Spirit who dwells in you" (Romans 8:11).

Yes, it is the will of God to heal you. Jesus said, "For I have come down from heaven, not to do My own will, but the will of Him who sent Me" (John 6:38). Watch Him as He opens the blind eyes and deaf ears, makes cripples leap for joy, and heals sick multitudes. What is He doing? *He is doing the will of God!*

If sickness is of God, then Jesus fought against His Father by healing the sick. Jesus said, "He who has seen Me has seen the Father" (John 14:9). Jesus wanted to show you what God's will was about sickness—*He healed them all.* How could it be more clear? Let God be true and every man a liar.

James 5:14–16 gives instructions about ministering to the sick. "Is *anyone* among you sick? Let him call for the elders of the church." If it is not the will of God to heal all, how could he say *any* sick? It is God's will, so *any* sick person can expect healing.

As I sought out more on this subject, I read the Psalms. I saw David pick up his harp and begin to sing: "Bless the LORD, O my soul, and forget not all His benefits: who forgives all your iniquities, who heals all your diseases" (Psalm 103:2–3).

I had always believed Jesus died for my sins, but I discovered He also died for my sicknesses. Matthew 8:17 states, "He Himself took our infirmities and bore our sicknesses." Praise the Name of the Lord!

Just as was true of the leper, I had settled the question. We presented our afflicted baby to God, *knowing* it was His will to heal her. We were no longer double minded on it. We did what the leper did and received what he did from the Lord—healing for our daughter! The doctor knows today that God performed a miracle in our child and healed her completely. She graduated from college and today she is a minister of the Gospel.

Face the Facts

Stop hugging your sickness as though it were a gift from God! "Let this mind be in you, which was also in Christ Jesus" (Philippians 2:5). Christ died for your sicknesses! You are free! Satan has no legal right to afflict your body! The prison door is open! Walk out in Jesus' Name!

Let's face the facts. If sickness is the will of God, then every physician is a lawbreaker, every trained nurse is defying the Almighty, and every hospital is a house of rebellion instead of a house of mercy. Instead of supporting hospitals, would we not do our utmost to close them?

If it is not the will of God, why did Jesus command the disciples to heal the sick?

If it is not the will of God, why did Jesus say, "And these signs will follow those who believe . . . they will lay hands on the sick, and they will recover" (Mark 16:17–18)?

If it is not the will of God, Jesus should not have said, "Whatever things you ask when you pray, believe that you receive them, and you will have them" (Mark 11:24).

If it is not the will of God to heal, we ought not to seek healing by any means—natural or supernatural. "Every good gift and every perfect gift is from above, and comes down from the Father of lights, with whom there is no variation or shadow of turning" (James 1:17).

If it is not the will of God to heal, then Jesus violated His Father's will because He healed people everywhere He went.

Praise the Lord, we know from the Word that it is the will of God to heal *all* the sick, which includes *you*. And we know that we should do all we can to get well. We need to take care of our bodies and seek medical help. Our oldest son, Paul, is a surgeon, and he told me once, "Daddy, we doctors can treat people, but only God can heal them."

Whatever promise from God's Word you are believing God for, you will not get what the leper did until you do what He did. Settle this matter in your heart. "It is the will of God for me."

WHEN THE HEALER COMES,

there is healing.

Reflection from
JOEL

*D*uring the late 1950s, my father was the successful pastor of a large congregation that had just built a brand-new sanctuary. But about that time, my sister Lisa was born with a birth injury, something similar to cerebral palsy. That was one of the darkest hours of my parents' lives. They searched the Scriptures, and their eyes were opened to the message of healing. However, the idea of a contemporary, miracle-working God was not received well by the church, and my heartbroken father eventually left that church and had to start all over with ninety other people in an abandoned feed store.

In that dark time, Daddy kept doing what he knew was right. God was preparing him for greater things.

CHAPTER EIGHT

A Man *of* Faith Believes *for the* Big When He Sees *the* Little

After Elijah's servant told him that there was a little cloud on the horizon, Elijah told his servant, "Go and tell Ahab, 'Hitch up your chariot and go down before the rain stops you'" (1 Kings 18:44 NIV). The cloud out over the sea may have been little, but Elijah knew it was the beginning of a gusher rainstorm. He saw the little but believed for the big. He sent word to Ahab, "That little cloud out there is the size of a man's hand, but I'm telling you, it's a sign that God is moving. You'd better hurry to get out of the rain."

Your first sign of relief may seem so small, but keep saying what God says about your situation. At the first sign of victory, don't stop, back up, or retreat. It's a sign the battle has turned and the enemy is on the run. It's the time to boldly proclaim you'll not be denied. You will have all that God has promised you.

As demonstrated by Elijah, the sixth quality of a man of unwavering faith is that he believes for the big when he sees the little.

FAITH IS ACTING ON THE WORD

There is an interesting account in Matthew 9:1–8 of the healing of the paralytic man. The scribes were bound up in their religious tradition that no one but God could forgive, or for that matter heal. Their lack of faith kept them from believing God's Word for salvation and healing. But, below we read that the paralyzed man heard Jesus' words, believed His Word, and received his healing!

"So He got into a boat, crossed over, and came to His own city. Then behold, they brought to Him a paralytic lying on a bed. When Jesus saw their faith, He said to the paralytic, 'Son, be of good cheer; your sins are forgiven you.' And at once some of the scribes said within themselves, 'This Man blasphemes!' But Jesus, knowing their thoughts, said, 'Why do you think evil in your hearts? For which is easier, to say, "Your sins are forgiven you," or to say, "Arise and walk"? But that you may know that the Son of Man has power on earth to forgive sins'— then He said to the paralytic, 'Arise, take up your bed, and go to your house.' And he arose and departed to his house. Now when the multitudes saw it, they marveled and glorified God, who had given such power to men."

When the scribes thought that Jesus' offer of forgiveness of sins was blasphemy, it paralyzed their faith. But what did this paralytic man do? He *acted* on the Word of God. Jesus told him to *do* what he could not do before, and he did it!

In Luke 5, when Jesus commanded Peter to let down his nets for a catch of fish, Peter hesitated. He told Jesus he had fished in those waters all night and had caught nothing. Peter was an authority on fishing. It seemed useless to try again, but he gave a marvelous statement of faith: *"Nevertheless at Your word I will let down the net"* (Luke 5:5). When he acted on the word of Jesus, he got results.

I realize that people have discouraged you and authorities have given their verdicts. Will you, in the face of all this, say, "Nevertheless at Your word I will act"?

Faith is an act. Believing the Word is acting on the Word. Faith without works is dead (James 2:20). One translation says, "Faith without corresponding action is dead." It is not enough to talk your faith. To say you believe and not act as though you believe shows you have dead faith.

The Bible says, "When Jesus saw their faith . . ." (Mark 2:5). Faith is something you can see. If you substitute the phrase *act on the Word* for *believe*, you will understand it more clearly.

"And these signs will follow those who believe [*act on My Word*]" (Mark 16:17). "He who believes in Me [*acts on My Word*], the works that I do he will do also; and greater *works* than these he will do, because I go to My Father" (John 14:12). "All things are possible to him who believes [*acts on My Word*]" (Mark 9:23).

Let's put it this way—*He who acts on the Word has!* That is present tense. When you act on the Word, you *have* whatsoever you desire of God. Hope is always in the future. Acting on the Word brings it to pass *now*.

Faith Is Acting as Though God Told You the Truth

The great men and women of the Old Testament never gave much thought to the matter of having faith. However, Hebrews 11 refers to them as mighty examples of faith. These men and women did not worry or fret about how to have faith. *They simply heard God speak and acted as though He told them the truth!*

How do I know that Noah believed? He started acting as though God told him the truth. He started building the ark (Genesis 6)! Joshua demonstrated his faith by marching around the walls of Jericho (Joshua 6). King

*Dare to believe
God's Word
and do what
circumstances
say you
cannot do!*

Jehoshaphat and his army showed their faith by beginning to sing and shout with joy (2 Chronicles 20). They acted as though God told them the truth.

How do I know this paralytic believed? When he heard Jesus say, "Arise," he acted as though he could and found out he was healed!

I saw this wonderful truth demonstrated in the city auditorium of Tulsa, Oklahoma. I was preaching about healing, and faith was building up in the hearts of the people. As they listened to the Word of God, they began to understand. Suddenly, I challenged them to do what they couldn't do before—right then—in the Name of Jesus! In the audience was a young girl who had a club foot. She accepted the challenge and attempted to stand normally on her crippled foot. Glory to God for His mercy! *She discovered it was absolutely normal!*

In a church in Houston, Texas, I prayed for an elderly woman who was badly afflicted with arthritis. She was stooped and hobbled along, using a cane. She could not lift her hands much higher than her waist. As she stood before me, I commanded the sickness to leave in the Name of Jesus! She hobbled away, seeming no better.

Three days later, as I continued the meetings, she started to come to the front again to be prayed for. I told her not to come, because she had been healed. She had been delivered because God promised to keep His Word. When I said these things, she turned and hobbled back to her seat.

After a few minutes, a commotion began in the audience. I looked and saw a cane waving in the air. The elderly lady had decided to act as though she was healed. She started running up and down the aisle and around the church with her arms high in the air. *When she acted, God kept His Word and she was healed!*

In one of our citywide campaigns, a pastor and I made a visit to a home to pray for a woman who had injured her back. She had lost her sense of balance and could not stand or walk without falling over. She was flat on her back in bed, and whenever she opened her eyes, she said the room would go around in circles. This had been going on for about ten weeks.

Based upon James 5:14–15, we anointed her with oil and commanded the spirit of infirmity to leave. We said, "Be healed in the Name of Jesus." After we had laid hands on her, we fully expected her to recover. I asked her if she thought God meant what He said, and she said yes. Then I told her that people who had been healed had no business in bed. I said, "Rise up and walk in the Name of Jesus!" She looked at me quizzically, but realized I was serious. Up she came with a determination to act as though God told her the truth. She stumbled a little, but then started walking normally. When she *acted*, she was healed.

In crowds numbering into the multiplied thousands, we have watched the marvelous power of God work as people *acted their faith*. I have seen all manner of sickness and disease healed as people acted on God's Word.

DARE TO DO THE IMPOSSIBLE

Dare to do the impossible! Dare to believe God's Word and do what circumstances say you cannot do!

I read the story of a dog that wouldn't stop chasing cars, so its owner chained it to a tree. When the dog raced out after the next car, it jerked its head terribly, and after several more painful attempts gave up. He would simply walk to the end of the chain and stop. He was unhappy, but he knew it was impossible to go one step farther.

One day his master decided the dog had learned its lesson and unbuckled the chain from the collar. The dog, though, continued to walk out to his former limits and sit and long for freedom. Little did he know that all he had to do was to *take one step beyond what he felt was his limitation to discover his deliverance!*

Freed, but not free. Delivered, but not enjoying it.

Many of us are like that. For years we have had sicknesses, fears, and limitations. Bitter experiences, apart from God's power, have convinced us that we can do just so much and no more.

But now you have heard the Gospel and know the good news. Your Master came all the way from heaven to let the oppressed go free. He came to set the captives free. "And you shall know the truth, and the truth shall make you free" (John 8:32). He broke the power of Satan!

His living words now are: "Rise, take up your bed and walk." "Be made whole!" "Woman, you are loosed from your infirmity!"

But thousands sit looking sad, wishing for deliverance, when all they need to do is to take one step that seems impossible and discover that with God all things are possible!

You are free! You will discover it to be so by acting as though God told you the truth.

As a man of faith, begin now to act your faith. You will not waver. You will not fail. He who acts on the Word of God has his miracle.

Reflection from
JOEL

Too many people today are living with a victim mentality. They are so focused on what they've been through, complaining about how unfair it was, they don't realize they are dragging the pains of the past into the present. It's almost as though they get up each day and fill a big wheelbarrow with junk from the past and bring it into the new day.

Let go of that stuff! Your past does not have to poison your future. Just because you've been through some hurt and pain, or perhaps one or more of your dreams have been shattered, that doesn't mean God doesn't have another plan. God still has a bright future in store for you.

CHAPTER NINE

A Man *of* Faith Begins With Nothing *but* Ends Up Doing Mighty Things

In the continuing story of the prophet Elijah and his servant that we have been studying, after all they went through, "The sky grew black with clouds, the wind rose, a heavy rain came on and Ahab rode off to Jezreel. The power of the LORD came on Elijah and, tucking his cloak into his belt, he ran ahead of Ahab all the way to Jezreel" (1 Kings 18:45–46 NIV).

As demonstrated by Elijah, the seventh quality of a man of unwavering faith is that he may begin with nothing, but he'll end up with the hand of God upon him, enabling him to do mighty exploits because of what he's seen God do in the hour of his trial of faith.

Elijah never gave up. He started with nothing, and he kept praying and believing until he saw the hand-size cloud. He kept on believing until the rain came, and then, the Bible states, the hand of God came upon him, and he ran across the Valley of Jezreel. He outran the horses of Ahab! Elijah experienced the victory because he endured the test of faith. He didn't give up.

Have you been tempted to give up? I want to tell you, there are good days ahead of you. I see you running with the hand of God on you. I see you walking in victory in your spiritual life.

Fight on! Believe the Word of God. Don't give up, because victory is just ahead of you.

Faith That Causes Jesus to Marvel

One of the greatest men of faith in the Bible was the Roman centurion who came to Jesus for the healing of his servant. If you do what he did by faith, you will receive what you need from God.

"Now when Jesus had entered Capernaum, a centurion came to Him, pleading with Him, saying, 'Lord, my servant is lying at home paralyzed, dreadfully tormented.' And Jesus said to him, 'I will come and heal him.' The centurion answered and said, 'Lord, I am not worthy that You should come under my roof. *But only speak a word, and my servant will be healed.* For I also am a man under authority, having soldiers under me. And I say to this one, "Go," and he goes; and to another, "Come," and he comes; and to my servant, "Do this," and he does it.' When Jesus heard it, He marveled, and said to those who followed, 'Assuredly, I say to you, I have not found such great faith, not even in Israel! And I say to you that many will come from east and west, and sit down with Abraham, Isaac, and Jacob in the kingdom of heaven. But the sons of the kingdom will be cast out into outer darkness. There will be weeping and gnashing of teeth.' Then Jesus said to the centurion, *'Go your way; and as you have believed, so let it be done for you.' And his servant was healed that same hour*" (Matthew 8:8–13).

What did the centurion do that caused Jesus to marvel? He said, *"But only speak a word, and my servant will be healed."*

He said in plain language, "I do not need the actual physical presence of Jesus. All I need is His spoken Word. If I have His spoken Word, I will believe it whether I see Jesus or not." Jesus responded by stating that He had not found such great faith in all Israel!

Faith is acting on the spoken Word of the Lord.

We have the spoken Word—*the Bible.* The centurion was willing to take the *words* of Jesus at face value. You will receive what he did when you are willing to do the same.

The centurion said in effect, "If Jesus says my servant is healed, that settles it for me. He is healed! No more worrying!"

Somebody near the centurion may have said, "But . . . what about the symptoms?" I hear him laugh them off with the words, "Those things are unreliable. I have the Word of the One who cannot lie. My servant shall live!"

Many people admire the Word, study the Word, and defend the Word, but they will not act on it as truth.

In this case, a man stepped out in faith on the spoken Word of Jesus. Will you do the same? Will you act on the Word God has given?

Isn't the Word of Jesus enough? Why are you worried? Do you think God has lied to you? Do you think His Word is no good? Face the facts. Either God lied or He told you the truth!

The Way You Act Reveals What You Believe

As I mentioned previously, when we prayed for our daughter, who was born with a crippling disease similar to cerebral palsy, we could see no change in her, but we *thanked* God for healing her. On what basis? Certainly not our five senses. Our eyes told us the opposite. The only basis we had was the Word of God. God kept His Word! *He always does!* "I am ready to perform My word" (Jeremiah 1:12).

When the widow of Zarephath obeyed the word of the Lord and prepared a cake for the prophet Elijah, she had

Many people admire the Word, study the Word, and defend the Word, but they will not act on it as truth.

nothing and was preparing to gather some sticks and cook her last meal and die with her son! Based upon the promise that the "bin of flour shall not be used up, nor shall the jar of oil run dry, until the day the LORD sends rain on the earth" (1 Kings 17:14), she went ahead despite the physical evidence and fixed her last meal for the man of God. As a result, every day throughout that famine she experienced miracles of provision.

Jesus said, "Whatever things you ask when you pray, believe that you receive them, and you will have them" (Mark 11:24). He said to believe it right when you pray—while you can still see the swelling, feel the fear and anxiety, and are conscious of all the symptoms. *Believe what God said right in the face of all contrary sense knowledge, and you shall have the things for which you asked Him.*

There are still signs of life in a tree immediately after it has been cut down. We do not worry because we know it has been cut down and all these signs of life will pass away in due time. When the Lord has cut down your disease, insecurity, or poverty, it is dead. Some of the symptoms may linger to convince you it is still alive and God has failed, but you know better. You confess the Word. You say what God says! The symptoms cry out that nothing has changed, but you stand with God. You confess what is true. You believe *when you pray* that you have received. God said that if you will believe His Word against all these other things, you shall have your request! When you have no basis for your victory but the Word of God, that is *real faith!*

Confess what God says!

You may say, "If I could only see a little change." Faith is the evidence of things *not seen*. You don't see your victory with your natural eyes, but with your spiritual eyes of faith. That evidence is from One who cannot lie. You have the Word of God.

The Seen and the Unseen

In Mark 11:12–24, Jesus rebuked a fig tree, but nothing happened immediately. I can imagine Peter and John lingering behind to see what happens to the tree. As they wait, they grow more and more disappointed. *Nothing about the tree has changed.* I can hear Peter say,

"John, Jesus has performed many miracles, but I believe He failed this time. I can't see any change."

The next day, however, they were amazed to see the tree dried up from the roots (Mark 11:20).

There are two parts to that tree—the *seen* and the *unseen*. Peter could see the outer part of the tree, but he couldn't see the root system, which is the source of the tree's life.

Now here is something to always remember. The withering, powerful, prevailing, authoritative Word of Jesus had its first effect in the realm Peter couldn't see—the life of the tree. If Peter could have seen as Jesus saw, he would have known at the instant He spoke that *the roots withered and died!*

In the realm you cannot see, God is working. The apostle Paul said, "For our light affliction, which is but for a moment, is working for us a far more exceeding and eternal weight of glory, while we do not look at the things which are seen, but at the things which are not seen. For the things which are seen are temporary, but the things which are not seen are eternal" (2 Corinthians 4:17–18).

As the centurion did, take Jesus at His Word! Believe He told you the truth! Act as though He told you the truth!

When our son Paul was a little boy, he had warts all

over his body. My wife, Dodie, tried in every way she knew to treat them so they would go away. It dawned on her one day that she could pray for him to be healed. She laid her hands on him and commanded the life of those warts to leave in the Name of Jesus. She knew the Word of God had taken effect in the unseen realm, though the warts still could be seen clearly. We looked at them day by day and said in the face of their continued presence, "Paul is healed in the Name of Jesus." We rejoiced and praised God that Paul was healed. About two weeks later, our son came in all excited. Several of the warts had disappeared. Soon all of them were gone!

We received what the centurion did because we did what he did—we believed and confessed the Word of God.

The Bible states, "My son, give attention to my words; incline your ear to my sayings. Do not let them depart from your eyes; keep them in the midst of your heart; for they are life to those who find them, and health to all their flesh" (Proverbs 4:20–22).

The man of unwavering faith ends up doing mighty exploits for God!

Reflection from
JOEL

When my father died back in 1999, I knew deep inside that I was to pastor Lakewood Church, but all I could see were the gigantic reasons why I couldn't do it. I thought, God, I don't feel qualified. I have only preached once. I've never been to seminary. I had to decide whether I was going to shrink back into my comfort zone or step out in faith, knowing that Almighty God was on my side.

I decided to go with God, but it wasn't easy. Several Sunday mornings I got up and thought, I can't do this! But I'd go stand before the mirror, look myself right in the eyes, and say, "Joel, you can do it in the power of God's might." I did it, and you can as well.

CHAPTER TEN

Faith *for* Our Families *and* Friends

As men of faith, we have Jesus' clear command to go into all the world and preach the Gospel to every creature, "that repentance and remission of sins should be preached in His name to all nations, beginning at Jerusalem" (Luke 24:47). We've always placed a major emphasis on the Great Commission at Lakewood Church and always will.

But notice that Jesus states the beginning point is *at Jerusalem*, which means where you live. In essence, Jesus was saying, "Certainly, My heart is to reach every nation. But if you don't first reach your Jerusalem, you won't do much for the rest of the world."

Song of Solomon 1:6 says, "They made me the keeper of vineyards, but my own vineyard I have not kept." God has made us keepers of vineyards. What is our *vineyard*? Our families, our friends, our neighborhoods, and our associates. We're not going to keep other vineyards and forget our own vineyard. As men of unwavering faith, we're going to have faith for our families and friends!

Yes, God has commanded us to go into all the world with the Gospel, but never at the expense of neglecting our own families. Oh, what a condemnation would come over us if we must confess that "my own vineyard I have not kept"!

What if I won the whole rest of the world to Jesus and neglected my own family? I can't fathom even one of my children dying without their faith being in Christ. Or my daddy, my mother, my nephews and nieces, or an old friend. God has made me a keeper of my family, and I am responsible to be a godly example and watch over them and pray for them.

Occasionally, someone will say to me, "Well, you know, I'm just not going to influence my child as to what religion is right. He needs to grow up and make his own choices."

How ridiculous is that? The world is influencing your child—the drug culture, pornography, television, the entertainment world, and liberal thinking in the school! It's time for us to rise up and bring our faith to our own families!

Perhaps you have read the book *Acres of Diamonds*

by Russell H. Conwell. It's the story about a man who had such an insatiable desire to find diamonds that he sold his property and went off to search for them. He traveled all over the world but never found any diamonds. Meanwhile, the new owner of his home discovered that a rich diamond mine was located right in the backyard of the man's property. Conwell's message to his audience: "Dig in your own backyard!"

I heartily support those who desire to take the Gospel to all of the world. But I'm telling you, the greatest treasure you have in the world is in your own backyard— your own wife and children and extended family. That is your own vineyard.

In Malachi 3:17, God said, "'They shall be Mine,' says the LORD of hosts, 'on the day that I make My jewels . . .'" I hope you realize your children and wife are diamonds for God. Treasure them!

"We Will Serve the Lord"

Let me ask you this. If you were charged with the crime of being a Christian, would there be enough evidence to convict you? Do your neighbors know you belong to Jesus? Your children? Your other family members?

The Word of God is repeatedly clear regarding the bringing of our faith to our families and our neighbors:

"Therefore you shall lay up these words of mine in your heart and in your soul, and bind them as a sign on your hand, and they shall be as frontlets between your eyes. You shall teach them to your children, speaking of them when you sit in your house, when you walk by the way, when you lie down, and when you rise up. And you shall write them on the doorposts of your house and on your gates" (Deuteronomy 11:18–20).

After Joshua had led the people of Israel into the Promised Land and was apportioning the land to the people, he declared, *"As for me and my house, we will serve the LORD"* (Joshua 24:15). As men of faith, we need to stand up and declare the same.

Will you stand up? Where are the men who are embracing their responsibilities as husbands and fathers, bringing their faith to their families day in and day out? Where are the daddies who take time for their sons and daughters rather than work, work, work, because of the love of money? Listen, making money is not the most important thing in the world. Making a life is. You can make money without making a life.

Has your child ever heard you say one thing about Jesus to them? Do you read the Word and pray with them? Have you ever put your hands on them and prayed for their healing? Have your children ever seen you hold

Do not discount the power of your faith and influence. It's amazing what one person who's saved can do in a household.

your wife's hand and bow your head in humility before God and seek His face? Oh, how important it is for the man to take the charge of his household and say with Joshua, "I don't know what the others are going to do, but as for me, my wife, and our children, we will serve the Lord!"

"GO HOME TO YOUR FRIENDS AND TELL THEM . . ."

Mark 5 records the remarkable story of Jesus casting the demons out of the man called Legion, "who had his dwelling among the tombs; and no one could bind him, not even with chains, because he had often been bound with shackles and chains. And the chains had been pulled apart by him, and the shackles broken in pieces; neither could anyone tame him. And always, night and day, he was in the mountains and in the tombs, crying out and cutting himself with stones" (vv. 3–5).

After the deliverance, we are told

that the man was sitting clothed at the feet of Jesus and in his right mind. "And when He got into the boat, he who had been demon-possessed begged Him that he might be with Him. However, Jesus did not permit him, but said to him, *'Go home to your friends, and tell them what great things the Lord has done for you, and how He has had compassion on you.'* And he departed and began to proclaim in Decapolis all that Jesus had done for him; and all marveled" (vv. 18–20).

When the man begged Jesus that he might go with Him, Jesus said, "No, I want you to go home. You've been demon-possessed, running around naked, living in the graveyard, trying to commit suicide, coming home bloody. Your children know it; your wife knows it; your neighbors know it; the whole city knows about it. You need to go home and tell them all the great things the Lord has done for you!" Which is precisely what he did, and it caused the people of Decapolis to "marvel"!

As men of faith, we believe God for our loved ones: our boys, our girls, our aunts, our uncles, our relatives, our neighbors—our own vineyard. We must do something about our own vineyard.

You may be the only one who can stand in faith for your family circle.

Unfortunately, too many men today are bound in a

manner like the demon-possessed man. Some are bound by anger and violence. Some are bent on destruction. Others are addicted to drugs or alcohol or pornography. That's what the devil does, and no man can deliver himself.

But now notice what Jesus can do. The demoniac saw Jesus afar off and the demons in him cried out, "Don't torment us before the time!" The demons were afraid in the presence of Jesus. And Jesus commanded those demons to come out.

All we have to have is Jesus. I want you to know there's no one who is beyond the touch of Jesus! That's what Jesus can do. He can bring you to calmness and tranquility, and you'll be sitting at His feet. He'll give you a sound mind so that you can think straight and live right.

Go back to your wife, your children, your mother, your daddy, whoever is at your home. They know what kind of man you've been. They know the torment you've been in. Go home to where you live! And don't just stop with your home; go to all your friends who were aware of your condition. Go to your home and to your friends and do two things: Tell them what great things the Lord has done for you and tell them that He has had compassion upon you!

But don't just tell them what God's done for you;

tell them about His compassion. You know it's hard for anyone who has lived a life of sin to believe that God loves them. But Christ came into this world for sinners; He died for sinners; He paid the sinner's price by going to hell in their place, and God raised Him from the dead. God loves everybody! He has no favorites.

We must tell people of the compassionate, loving heart of God. He loves them! He wants them, and He needs them. And they're welcome in the kingdom of God.

But praying is not enough. You've got to go and tell.

OUR SUFFICIENCY IS GOD

In Acts 27, Paul was in a storm at sea that was so bad that those on the ship hadn't seen the sun or the stars for fourteen days. Finally, the Bible says, "All hope that we would be saved was finally given up." All hope in the natural realm was gone.

And yet in the midst of the hopelessness, Paul had an angel appear to him who said, "Do not be afraid, Paul; you must be brought before Caesar; and indeed God has granted you all those who sail with you" (v. 24). All hope was gone, yet every one of them was saved.

If you have a situation and all hope is gone, you can turn it around with Jesus so that everything will turn out all right! God never sent that storm, but He invaded that storm and directed its winds. He said, "Oh, you're trying to kill my servant Paul? I'll tell you what I'll do. I'll direct the winds of this storm, and I'll put Paul over there on the island called Malta, which is filled with suffering sick people. Everyone on that island is going to come to know the healing power of the Lord Jesus Christ!"

You may be in a storm today. God never sent it, but He will invade it. Let Him come in. Let Him direct it, and you'll find that in the storm, you'll reach your island of needs, your dreams. Let your storm cause you to bend your knees and look away from man unto God. Let your storm make you realize that you're not sufficient in yourself! Our sufficiency is of God!

Live as a Shining Light

"Live clean, innocent lives as children of God, shining like bright lights in a world full of crooked and perverse people" (Philippians 2:15 NLT).

In Acts 16 is the marvelous story of the apostle Paul who cast a demon out of a young woman who was a soothsayer. But the result of Paul's actions was that an angry mob got together and the magistrates were called out. They punished Paul and Silas, stripping their backs bare and beating them unmercifully. Then they took them to the jail and charged the jailer to keep them safe.

He threw them into the inner dungeon and put their feet fast in the stocks.

Then the Bible says, "Suddenly there was a great earthquake, so that the foundations of the prison were shaken; and immediately all the doors were opened and everyone's chains were loosed. And the keeper of the prison, awaking from sleep and seeing the prison doors open, supposing the prisoners had fled, drew his sword and was about to kill himself. But Paul called with a loud voice, saying, 'Do yourself no harm, for we are all here.' Then he called for a light, ran in, and fell down trembling before Paul and Silas. And he brought them out and said, *'Sirs, what must I do to be saved?'* So they said, *'Believe on the Lord Jesus Christ, and you will be saved, you and your household.'* Then they spoke the word of the Lord to him and to all who were in his house. And he took them the same hour of the night and washed their stripes. And immediately he and all his family were baptized. Now when he had brought them into his house, he set food before them; and he rejoiced, having believed in God with all his household" (vv. 26–34).

At midnight, Paul and Silas were in the stocks with their backs bleeding, and they prayed and sang praises to God! Anybody can sing when the sun shines, but a real Christian can sing whatever is happening. It may be dark around you, but it's light on the inside. *When you have revelation knowledge in you; when you know who you are; when you know how it's all going to come out in the end, you can praise God in the darkness.* If you'll praise Him in the darkness, He'll bring you out into the sunshine!

When Paul prevented the jailer from taking his own life, the jailer's immediate reaction was to fall before Paul and Silas and ask, "Sirs, what must I do to be saved?" The testimony of Paul and Silas was so clear that the jailer desperately wanted the life of Jesus for himself and his household. The jailer was saying, "I want to be like you. I want to have the joy you have. I want to have the victory you have. I want to have that something you have."

Paul's answer was simple and clear: "Believe on the Lord Jesus Christ." Not believe just *in* Jesus, but *on* Him. Trust yourself to Him. Commit your whole life to Him as your Lord and Savior, and you shall be saved. And then here's what I'm talking about, *"And your household!"* It's not just good for Daddy; it's good for the whole house!

And so, the Bible says they preached the Word of God to the jailer and all his household, who all came to saving faith in God. Then the Bible says the jailer rejoiced much. One translation says he leaped for joy with all his house, because they believed in God! Four times it states *"all your house."* So God wants our households saved!

It was an earthquake that brought the jailer to God. God does not send sorrow and trouble and heartache and cancer and AIDS and all of that. Great tragedies happen every day. God is not the author of all of that. But earthquakes can bring us to God! And sometimes it has to be allowed in order to shake us to our foundation.

You may be going through great trouble, an earthquake, right now. You say it's worse than anything you can imagine, and you don't know what you're going to do. Let it drive you to your knees. Commit yourself to God.

You might ask, "Well, will God do for me what he did for the jailer?" God will do anything for this world! He'll send laborers across your path. He'll send angels to warn you. He'll appear to you. With God all things are possible!

Let's believe for every nation to be shaken by the power of God, but let's also believe for our own families and friends and neighborhoods and schools. We must get the violence and the drugs and the pornography out of our young people, and we must set them free. We must get our fathers committed to Jesus and our mothers living for Him, and then our cities will be changed!

You need to shout, "My household shall be saved!" Say it again! "My household shall be saved!"

Do not discount the power of your faith and influence.

It's amazing what one person who's saved can do in a household. See how the jailer who got saved asked Paul to come and preach to his household, and everyone in his household got baptized. It's amazing what one saved person who lets his or her light shine can do for Jesus!

When I first put my faith in Christ, my entire household went to nightclubs and was living for the world. I was a little timid and wasn't sure what to say to them, but instead of going out with them, I'd stay home and get out the big old family Bible and read it. I didn't understand much of what I read, but I was trying to let my light shine.

One night my sister Mary was going out to a nightclub and came and stood right beside me. Then she said, "John, why do you stay home and read the Bible now and don't go out with us?" I didn't look up, but I said, "Mary, I've given my heart to Jesus, and I'm not going to the world anymore!" I thought she'd pounce on me, but nothing came out of her mouth. So I looked up, and tears were running down her face. She said, "John, do you think Jesus would save somebody like me?" I said, "Oh, Mary, He will. He will." In that moment, Mary knelt at the dining room table and passed out of darkness into light, out of death into eternal life.

And one by one the other members of my family came

to faith. Mother got saved. My other sister came running in one night and said, "I was in a tent revival, and I gave my heart to Jesus." My brother gave his heart to the Lord. Daddy wasn't so easy. He said, "When you're dead, you're dead like a dog. Roll me over in a ditch. That's all there is to life." I said, "Daddy, if that were true, I'll never bother you again. But you've got to live on forever somewhere." Thank God, he got saved!

As men of unwavering faith, let us let our light shine! It's wonderful what one light can do!

WE MUST TELL PEOPLE OF

THE COMPASSIONATE, LOVING HEART OF GOD.

He loves them!

Reflection from
JOEL

Nobody could have represented the goodness of God any better to us Osteen kids than my dad did. Even when we made mistakes or got off track, while Daddy was firm, he was also loving and kind. He nurtured us back to the right course. He never beat us into line; he loved us onto the right path. Although he was very busy, he always took time for us. He encouraged us to do great things, to fulfill our dreams.

If you are a father, you need to realize that most children get their concepts of who God is and what He is like from their fathers. If the father is mean, critical, and harsh, inevitably the children will grow up with a distorted view of God. If the father is loving, kind, compassionate, and just, the children will better understand God's character.

CHAPTER ELEVEN

The Message God Entrusts *to* Men *of* Faith

"Praise the LORD! Blessed is the man who fears the LORD, who delights greatly in His commandments. His descendants will be mighty on earth; the generation of the upright will be blessed. Wealth and riches will be in his house, and his righteousness endures forever. He will not be afraid of evil tidings; his heart is steadfast, trusting in the LORD. His heart is established; he will not be afraid, until he see his desire upon his enemies" (Psalm 112:1–3, 7–8).

These are tough days when most men live in dread, worry, and anxiety. But if we are greatly delighting in the commandments of the Lord, we don't have to live in dread. We are settled that Jehovah God will take care of us. It's settled. It's written.

Beyond that, though, as men of faith, our deep concern must be in reaching our family, our friends, our neighbors, and telling them about Jesus so we can take them to heaven with us.

In Acts 10:1–5 is a marvelous story of God's compassion on a man who was concerned about his house. Here is a man whose heart shares the interests of God's heart—that his entire household and neighbors would come to faith in Christ!

"There was a certain man in Caesarea called Cornelius, a centurion of what was called the Italian Regiment, a devout man and one who feared God with all his household, who gave alms generously to the people, and prayed to God always. About the ninth hour of the day he saw clearly in a vision an angel of God coming in and saying to him, 'Cornelius!' And when he observed him, he was afraid, and said, 'What is it, lord?' So he said to him, 'Your prayers and your alms have come up for a memorial before God. Now send men to Joppa, and send for Simon whose surname is Peter.'" Then in Acts 11:14, it continues the statement regarding Peter: "Who will tell you words by which you and all your household will be saved."

This man was like so many people who are religious and do many good things. He was a devout man who feared God, gave away much alms, and prayed to God always but did not have a relationship with Jesus. He needed Peter to come and lead him into the way of salvation. He knew about God, but he didn't really know God.

But this seeking man does not go unnoticed by God, who was so moved by this man's reaching toward Him that He sent an angel to him. The angel said to him, "Your prayers and your giving has come up to God for a memorial." God hears the cry and the prayer of men.

The angel told the centurion to send for Simon Peter to come tell him the words whereby he and his household could be saved. In the meantime, despite the fact that it was ten years after Jesus said to go into all the world and preach the Gospel to every person, Peter needed a vision of his own to convince him to go to Cornelius, because Cornelius was a Gentile, and the Jews had no dealings with Gentiles. Racial prejudice was a deeply embedded issue in the life of the early Church as a carryover from their past, and Peter wasn't perfect.

So God first got Peter ready, and when Peter met Cornelius's household, he told him these words that we as men of faith need to incorporate into our lives as we reach out to our loved ones:

"Then Peter opened his mouth and said: 'In truth I perceive that God shows no partiality. But in every nation whoever fears Him and works righteousness is accepted by Him. The word which God sent to the children of Israel, preaching peace through Jesus Christ—He is Lord of all—that word you know, which was proclaimed throughout all Judea, and began from Galilee after the baptism which John preached: how God anointed Jesus of Nazareth with the Holy Spirit and with power, who went about doing good and healing all who were oppressed by the devil, for God was with Him. And we are witnesses of all things which He did both in the land of the Jews and in Jerusalem, whom they killed by hanging on a tree. Him God raised up on the third day, and showed Him openly, not to all the people, but to witnesses chosen before by God, even to us who ate and drank with Him after He arose from the dead. And He commanded us to preach to the people, and to testify that it is He who was ordained by God to be Judge of the living and the dead. To Him all the prophets witness that, through His name, whoever believes in Him will receive remission of sins'" (Acts 10:34–44).

I see seven principles in these ten verses that I believe every man of faith needs to know.

1. GOD HAS NO FAVORITES

"I perceive that God shows no partiality" (v. 34).

What a glorious Gospel you can share with and live out before your family and neighbors. Go out and tell them that God is a good God.

The first basic principle is that God has no favorites. He is no respecter of persons. He loves the prostitute just as much as He loves the virgin. He loves the alcoholic just as much as He loves the sober man. God doesn't respect the color of your skin. God doesn't respect the social standing that you have. God loves everybody the same way.

God is no respecter of persons, and that's where we need to start. This is crucial, because we may have a hard time believing that some of our loved ones, relatives, and neighbors can come to faith because of the way they've lived. Those same people may also believe they can't get saved because of the way they've lived, so we have to make them realize God is no respecter of persons.

2. GOD ACCEPTS YOU

"But in every nation whoever fears Him and works righteousness is accepted by Him" (v. 35).

This represents the all-encompassing acceptance of Jesus for every nation and every person in every nation, which includes your own family and neighbors. Everyone has the same opportunity for faith.

3. Peace Comes Only Through Jesus

"The word which God sent to the children of Israel, preaching peace through Jesus Christ—He is Lord of all" (v. 36).

The third principle is that peace comes by Jesus Christ, and Jesus is Lord! There is no way to get peace of heart except through Jesus. You can't buy it, sniff it, shoot it, drink it, or manufacture it. The only way in the world you can have peace of heart and lie down at night knowing everything is right between you and God is through Jesus Christ.

4. God Is a Good God

"How God anointed Jesus of Nazareth with the Holy Spirit and with power, who went about doing good and healing all who were oppressed by the devil, for God was with Him" (v. 38).

Just as Peter did, we must tell people that God sent His only Son into the world. Jesus was born of a virgin and lived His life doing good, demonstrating the goodness and the mercy of God. He went into every city and every village, healed every sickness and every disease among the people. He stood by the woman caught in adultery and lifted her up (John 8). Jesus brought the despised Samaritan woman who had been married five times, living with a man to whom she wasn't even married, to salvation and reached out to her entire village (John 4). He sought out Zacchaeus who didn't feel worthy to even come into His presence (Luke 19). He reached out to the bad and the good alike, constantly demonstrating God's love by doing good. Tell people that God is a good God.

5. Jesus Bore Your Sin on the Cross

"We are witnesses of all things which He did both in the land of the Jews and in Jerusalem, whom they killed by hanging on a tree . . ." (v. 39).

The fifth principle is that we must tell our loved ones that Jesus was crucified in their place. He didn't know sin. The reason He went to the cross was He was bearing our immorality, our anger, our stealing, and our sins of all kind. He bore our sins. We must tell them that Jesus came to pay the price. He died on that cross and paid the price of God's judgment so we can be free of sin and shame and guilt. (See 1 Peter 2:24.)

6. Jesus Died for You

"Him God raised up on the third day, and showed Him openly, not to all the people, but to witnesses chosen before by God, even to us who ate and drank with Him after He arose from the dead" (vv. 40–41).

God raised Jesus from the dead. On the third day, a mighty angel rolled the stone away—not to let Jesus out, but so the disciples could get in and see that He'd already risen from the dead! Resurrection power came upon Jesus, and He was raised from the dead, and His body was glorified as a human body. Then He went down into Satan's domain and approached the devil as the risen Conqueror of death, taking the crown from his head and taking the keys of death from him.

Read in Revelation 1 where Jesus stands as brilliant as the sun pulsating with eternal glory. Jesus died on the cross and paid the price for our salvation. He said, "I am He who lives, and was dead; and, behold, I am alive forevermore. Amen. And have the keys of Hades and of death" (Revelation 1:18).

We've got to tell people that Jesus died for them! And He arose for them! Thank God! That's what He did. He arose from the dead! These are words whereby salvation is delivered.

"And He commanded us to preach to the people, and to testify that it is He who was ordained by God to be Judge of the living and the dead" (v. 42).

As men of faith, Jesus commanded us to take this news all over the world. Everybody has a right to hear this message, and we must do our part to deliver it. The fact is that one day every knee shall bow to Jesus and every tongue will confess that He is Lord (Philippians 2:10–11). God has ordained that Jesus will judge the living and dead. Every man, woman, and child will stand before Jesus.

Jesus said, "And I, if I am lifted up from the earth, will draw all peoples to Myself" (John 12:32). We tend to misinterpret this scripture. We say, "Well, if we just lift up Jesus, people will come to Him." Yes, that's true in a sense, but that isn't what Jesus meant. He was saying, "If I go ahead and obey the Father, and I die on that cross; if I bear their sins and their sicknesses; if I take their judgment and pay the price and go down into hell; and if I rise again, I will draw every human being before Me."

Now Jesus is saying to us as men of faith, "What did you do with what I did for you? What did you do with Me? What attitude did you take about what I did?"

With every beat of your heart and every tick of the clock, you're getting closer to the time when you, your loved ones, and your neighbors will stand before Jesus, who is the Judge of the living and the dead. No man can remit your sins or their sins but Jesus. "To him give all the prophets witness, that through his name whosoever believeth in him shall receive remission of sins" (Acts 10:43 KJV). Whoever will believe on Jesus will receive not just forgiveness of sins but a remission of sins. *Remission* means that it's stamped "paid in full"!

What a glorious Gospel you can share with and live out before your family and neighbors. Go out and tell them that God is a good God.

JESUS IS SAYING TO US AS MEN OF FAITH,

"What did you do with what I did for you?"

Reflection from
JOEL

Because I grew up with acceptance and approval from my parents, now, as a father myself, I'm speaking words of blessing into my children's lives that will be passed down to another generation, and on and on. Before our children go to bed, Victoria and I tell them, "There's nothing you can't do. You have a bright future in front of you. You're surrounded by God's favor. Everything you touch is going to prosper." We believe we have an opportunity and a responsibility to speak God's blessings into our children now, while they are young.

Don't wait until your children are teenagers or in their twenties and about to get married to begin praying for God's blessings in their lives. No, declare God's blessings over them all the days of their lives, starting now.

CHAPTER TWELVE

What *to* Do When Nothing Seems *to* Work

Sooner or later, even as men of faith, we all come into a place where we are tempted to say, "It just does not look as though anything is going to work."

There is a touching situation in the Bible where nothing seemed to work when a needy man approached Jesus' disciples for help.

"And when they had come to the multitude, a man came to Him, kneeling down to Him and saying, 'Lord, have mercy on my son, for he is an epileptic and suffers severely; for he often falls into the fire and often into the water. So I brought him to Your disciples, but they could not cure him.' Then Jesus answered and said, 'O faithless and perverse generation, how long shall I be with you? How long shall I bear with you? Bring him here to Me.' And Jesus rebuked the demon, and it came out of him; and the child was cured from that very hour. Then the disciples came to Jesus privately and said, 'Why could we not cast it out?' So Jesus said to them, 'Because of your unbelief; for assuredly, I say to you, if you have faith as a mustard seed, you will say to this mountain, "Move from here to there," and it will move; and nothing will be impossible for you'" (Matthew 17:14–20).

Here is a father with a tremendous need. His son has severe seizures and suicidal actions. He brought his son to the best deliverance evangelists of that day—the ones who were directly trained under the ministry of Jesus. Yet after the disciples did everything they knew to do, every one of them failed.

There are times when nothing seems to work.

There Is Always Hope

Let me tell you, there is always hope when you are in trouble. The psalmist David said, "I will lift up my eyes to the hills—from whence comes my help?" (Psalm 121:1).

When that father lifted his eyes and looked, there was Jesus coming down the mountain! His face was still shining from His Transfiguration as He comes (Matthew 17:1–13). When He comes on the scene, every failure, every sickness, and every demon leaves.

All we need to do is get Jesus on the scene.

Jesus is the Living Word. There is the written Word,

and Jesus is that Word personified. "And the Word became flesh and dwelt among us, and we beheld His glory, the glory as of the only begotten of the Father, full of grace and truth" (John 1:14). If we can activate the Word of God in the midst of our failures, we can find help from God.

Jesus came down into this valley and asked the man what he was seeking from the disciples. The man told Him about his son, adding that the disciples had not been able to help his son. Jesus told the man to bring the boy to Him. "And Jesus rebuked the demon, and it came out of him; and the child was cured from that very hour" (Matthew 17:18).

This father found his answer in the Lord Jesus. He brought the Living Word to his situation.

Jesus is wonderful! We need to preach Jesus. This generation needs to see Jesus. If we can just give suffering, sighing, crying, dying humanity a glimpse of Jesus, Who is ever the same and Who has the power to perform whatever we need, people will run to Him. They will run to Him because He is still the marvelous Son of God as pictured in the Bible.

"Jesus Christ is the same yesterday, today, and forever" (Hebrews 13:8). He is with you wherever you go. He said, "And lo, I am with you always, even to the end of the age"

(Matthew 28:20). And He has said, "I will never leave you nor forsake you" (Hebrews 13:5).

As men of unwavering faith, we need to know what to do when we find ourselves in the valley and nothing is working. People pray and seek God for success, healing, and deliverance. They seek to move in the gifts of the Holy Spirit and for doors of ministry to open. They pray and pray and pray. They try every formula they have heard of, yet nothing seems to work.

We need Jesus in our valley. He will reveal the way, because He is the Way! He said, "I am the way, the truth, and the life" (John 14:6).

Years ago, I had a new car, one of the best, and I was so proud of it. But one day as I was approaching the highway, it abruptly stopped. The engine in my brand-new car would not even turn over. I was so disappointed, and I could have just walked off and left it there, concluding that it wouldn't work for me. But I knew this car was built to run, so I called my mechanic, who came and found that a little wire had gotten disconnected. Once the wire was connected, it started right away, and I went merrily on down the road.

You may get some wonderful teaching and truth from one of God's anointed teachers. You may jump at the opportunity to try it. You say, "It is so wonderful." All goes well as you drive it down the road, until you hit a problem. When you try to apply what you have learned, the whole operation fails. Then you say, "He said it would work, but I turned the key and nothing happened. It is in the Bible, but it is not working for me."

When nothing seems to work, you need Jesus to show you your loose connection. It isn't that the Bible does not work. *God's Word works!* We must realize that if there is something wrong, it is not with God or His Word; it may be us.

When you are seeking God, and you are believing faithfully and trying to apply God's Word to a situation, and nothing seems to work, here are some checkpoints to help you find your loose connection.

FIRST, CHECK UP ON YOUR OWN LIFE

When I face adversity, the first thing I do is to turn God's great searchlight on in my heart to check up on my own life. I want to find out if I have overlooked anything that needs to be made right. Jesus said, "And whenever you stand praying, if you have anything against anyone, forgive him, that your Father in heaven may also forgive you your trespasses" (Mark 11:25).

If I have any envy, strife, jealousy, wrath, or anything against anyone, I want to know it. I say, "Search me, O

God, and know my heart; try me, and know my anxieties" (Psalm 139:23).

I know that if I do not close up every gap, Satan would have an opportunity to enter in. He has no place unless we give him that place. The Bible says, "Nor give place to the devil" (Ephesians 4:27).

The patriarch Job had a hedge about him. The devil had to admit the truth to God in saying, "Have You not made a hedge around him, around his household, and around all that he has on every side?" (Job 1:10). A hedge is a wall that the devil cannot get through. But we find out God permitted Satan to trespass the hedge because Job allowed fear to come into his life. There was a gap. He said, "For the thing I greatly feared has come upon me, and what I dreaded has happened to me" (Job 3:25). Fear opened the door for Satan to come in and try to destroy him in the way that we see written in the Book of Job.

Check your own life. You have a hedge about you. Over you is the blood of Jesus Christ. Around you encamp the angels of the Lord. The Lord goes before you. Goodness and mercy are following you all the days of your life. Underneath are the Everlasting Arms.

That hedge about you can be broken by an unforgiving spirit, jealousy, envy, strife, stinginess, covetousness, lasciviousness, evil desire, immorality, lust, or unforgiven sin. Many times the hedge is broken down because of unresolved anger. "'Be angry, and do not sin': do not let the sun go down on your wrath" (Ephesians 4:26).

If God's Word is not working for you, check up on your own life first. Examine yourself (1 Corinthians 11:31).

"If it is possible, as much as depends on you, live peaceably with all men" (Romans 12:18). Forgive your wife. Forgive your children. Ask them to forgive you. The Word says, "And be kind to one another, tenderhearted, forgiving one another, even as God in Christ forgave you" (Ephesians 4:32).

Keep strife out of your life. God will not work for you while you live in open rebellion against His Word.

Second, Check Up on Your Promises

If you do not have some definite promise from the Word of God that has been whispered to your heart and which you have embraced; if you do not have any real, definite, pointed promise that God has quickened to you in your present situation, then you have a loose connection.

Get into God's Word. Meditate on the Scriptures until God speaks to your heart. "Be diligent to present yourself approved to God, a worker who does not need to be ashamed, rightly dividing the word of truth" (2 Timothy 2:15).

You cannot have faith for something unless you have a promise from God's Word. Check your Promise Book!

If you are believing God for finances, check up on the verses that apply. "Beloved, I pray that you may prosper in all things and be in health, just as your soul prospers" (3 John 2).

If you are believing for healing, check up on your healing scriptures. "Who Himself bore our sins in His own body on the tree, that we, having died to sins, might live for righteousness—by whose stripes you were healed" (1 Peter 2:24).

Whatever you are believing for, check your promises! *God's Word will never change! It will never fail!*

I have a missionary friend in Mexico who picked up a hitchhiker one day and began to talk with him about the Lord. The hitchhiker pulled a gun, pointed it at him, and told him to pull off onto a country road. This convict planned to take the car and everything in it and leave my friend in a deserted place.

My friend turned to this fellow and said, "You cannot do this to me. I have more power than you have. 'Greater is He that is in me than he that is in the world.'"

The convict said, "Drive."

My friend kept driving, feeling the gun jabbing in his side. But he said, "You cannot do this to me. The Bible says that I have all power over the devil, who is making you do this. You cannot do this to me."

The convict made him drive down a deserted road and stop. Then he got out of the car.

My friend persisted. "You cannot do this to me! I have Jesus in me. In the Name of Jesus, you cannot do this to me."

The convict directed him into a field and told him to take off his clothes. There stood my friend in his underwear. . . . God's man of unwavering faith and power!

It *really* looked as though it was not working and everything had failed.

As the convict walked away to the car, my friend lifted his voice one more time and shouted, "In the Name of Jesus you cannot do this. I command you in Jesus' Name to come back! Satan, you are defeated in Jesus' Name!"

In just a few moments, the convict came back, handed him his clothes, and said, "Hombre, I like you!"

There is power in the Name of Jesus! It may look as though the enemy is stripping you down to nothing, but if you will check on your promises and put your whole confidence in the Word of God, you will have the victory.

When once you get the Word of God settled in you, there will be no sickness, no poverty, no disease, no defeat, and no calamities, because the Word of God is forever settled in *you!*

You must settle it.

The Word of God will lift you into a higher realm of faith. "So then faith comes by hearing, and hearing by the word of God" (Romans 10:17).

Check up on your promises. Find out what God says. See if He has told you the truth. See if He still says what you think He says.

Did you put your confidence in His Word in the beginning? Did you have faith in Jesus before you were going through this valley? God's Word will not change.

Remind God and remind yourself of what God says.

Quit mumbling, murmuring, moaning, groaning, grumbling, and complaining. *Check your promises!*

Third, Check Up on Your Confession of Faith

Jesus said, "For assuredly, I say to you, whoever says to this mountain, 'Be removed and be cast into the sea,' and does not doubt in his heart, but believes that those things he says will be done, he will have whatever he says" (Mark 11:23).

You will never rise any higher than your confession. You will never sink any lower than your confession.

A lot of people have the idea that if they can just take God's Word in an emergency and quote it, it will work. It will not!

There is always hope when we are in trouble. All we need to do is get Jesus on the scene.

You will have whatsoever you say or whatsoever you have been saying continually. You cannot just talk any way you want to all the time and then suddenly quote God's Word and expect a miracle. It doesn't work that way.

You must train yourself to continually speak and believe God's Word and live it out daily.

Death and life are in the power of the tongue (Proverbs 18:21).

Check up on your words. Usually when you are having a problem, it is because you are not saying what God says about the situation. Instead, you are speculating, surmising, reasoning, and looking at the circumstances instead of God's Word. The Word of God says we are to be "casting down arguments and every high thing that exalts itself against the knowledge of God, bringing every thought into captivity to the obedience of Christ" (2 Corinthians 10:5).

If there are all kinds of contrary

thoughts in your mind, as long as you refuse to say those thoughts, they will die stillborn. Once you speak them, you give them life! Replace negative thoughts with God's thoughts—the Bible.

Meditate on God's Word. Say what God says about your situation.

Before you ever get out of bed in the morning, pray in the Holy Spirit. Confess what God's Word says about you. Know who you are in Christ. Pray the following prayers:

". . . that the God of our Lord Jesus Christ, the Father of glory, may give to you the spirit of wisdom and revelation in the knowledge of Him, the eyes of your understanding being enlightened; that you may know what is the hope of His calling, what are the riches of the glory of His inheritance in the saints, and what is the exceeding greatness of His power toward us who believe, according to the working of His mighty power which He worked in Christ when He raised Him from the dead and seated Him at His right hand in the heavenly places, far above all principality and power and might and dominion, and every name that is named, not only in this age but also in that which is to come. And He put all things under His feet, and gave Him to be head over all things to the church, which is His body, the fullness of Him who fills all in all" (Ephesians 1:17–23).

". . . that Christ may dwell in your hearts through faith; that you, being rooted and grounded in love, may be able to comprehend with all the saints what is the width and length and depth and height—to know the love of Christ which passes knowledge; that you may be filled with all the fullness of God. Now to Him who is able to do exceedingly abundantly above all that we ask or think, according to the power that works in us, to Him be glory in the church by Christ Jesus to all generations, forever and ever. Amen" (Ephesians 3:17–21).

FOURTH, CHECK UP ON THE ARENA IN WHICH YOU ARE FIGHTING

If the devil ever gets you in the arena of reasoning and looking at your symptoms, he will defeat you every time. Stay in the arena of faith and you will win every time.

Check up on the arena in which you are fighting. Are you trying to battle Satan in the arena of reason? Are you trying to intellectualize your problem? Are you battling symptoms and trying to reason why? *Stop!* Get into the realm of faith. Say this: "It does not matter what the situation looks like. It may look like these circumstances may never change, but Jesus said in Matthew 21:22, 'And all these things, whatsoever you shall ask in prayer, believing, you shall receive'" (quote His Word).

Believe God!

Fifth, Check Up on Your Companions and Fellowship

Are you in constant fellowship with people of faith? If you associate with people who cannot support you in faith, you may find yourself struggling to hold on to your promise.

You will become like the individuals with whom you associate. "Do not be misled: 'Bad company corrupts good character'" (1 Corinthians 15:33 NIV). Fellowship with men and women of faith. Of course, open your heart to all people and share the love of Jesus, but where you counsel and fellowship and when you listen and are exhorted, be sure you have chosen those who are established in the Word of God and in faith.

Your ears are not garbage cans! Mark 4:24 says, "Be careful what you are hearing. The measure [of thought and study] you give [to the truth you hear] will be the measure [of virtue and knowledge] that comes back to you—and more [besides] will be given to you who hear" (AMP).

Do not agree with unbelief and doubt. Do not counsel with people who bring reproach upon the Word of God.

Take your stand! Do what is right. Do not compromise God's Word. If somebody says something to you that will bring you down, answer with the Word of God.

The apostle Paul reminds us to find our fellowship with the people of God: "Let the word of Christ dwell in you richly in all wisdom, teaching and admonishing one another in psalms and hymns and spiritual songs, singing with grace in your hearts to the Lord" (Colossians 3:16).

Check up on your companions and fellowship.

Sixth, Check Up on Yourself to See if You Are Obeying the Scriptures

Many people live very worldly lives. They disregard the commandments of God. When they try to appropriate God's promises, they fail.

The Bible says, "Be anxious for nothing, but in everything by prayer and supplication, with thanksgiving, let your requests be made known to God" (Philippians 4:6).

"Put on the whole armor of God, that you may be able to stand against the wiles of the devil" (Ephesians 6:11).

You must know who you are in Christ so you can resist the schemes of the enemy.

"But be doers of the word, and not hearers only, deceiving yourselves. For if anyone is a hearer of the word and not a doer, he is like a man observing his natural face in a mirror; for he observes himself, goes away, and immediately forgets what kind of man he was. But he who looks into the perfect law of liberty and continues in it, and is not a forgetful hearer but a doer of the work, this one will be blessed in what he does" (James 1:22–25).

You must *do* the Word of God. It will not do you any good unless you obey the Word.

Jesus told this story about the men who built a house, one on a rock, the other on the sand: "Therefore whoever hears these sayings of Mine, and does them, I will liken him to a wise man who built his house on the rock: and the rain descended, the floods came, and the winds blew and beat on that house; and it did not fall, for it was founded on the rock. But everyone who hears these sayings of Mine, and does not do them, will be like a foolish man who built his house on the sand: and the rain descended, the floods came, and the winds blew and beat on that house; and it fell. And great was its fall" (Matthew 7:24–27).

The one house stood because that man was a doer of the Word.

When the Lord says, "Do not let the sun go down on your wrath" (Ephesians 4:26), you must obey. When the Lord says, "And be kind to one another" (Ephesians 4:32), you must obey. When the Lord says to "forgive" (Luke 6:37), you must forgive.

James 4:7 tells us, "Therefore submit to God. Resist the devil and he will flee from you." Make certain you are submitting all of your life to God.

As Peter did, obey Jesus when He speaks to your heart and say, "Nevertheless at Your word I will . . ." (Luke 5:5), even when it doesn't all make sense to you.

Seventh, Check Up on Your Praise Life

Are you showing your faith by praising God *before* you see the answer. The Word of God tells us: "I will bless the Lord at all times. His praise shall continually be in your mouth."

Check to see if you are praising God as if you already had your answer. If you will act like you have it, talk like you have it, praise God like you have it, *you will have it!*

Let me remind you of what I said previously. Jesus praised God that Lazarus was raised from the dead *before* He ever raised him. He stood before that grave and said, "Father, I thank You that You have heard Me. [I thank You that You have already raised him as far as I am concerned]" (John 11:41).

Somebody said, "I would be afraid to say that. Lazarus might not come out!" Certainly he would not come out with that attitude of doubt!

Joshua and the children of Israel shouted triumphantly

before the walls fell down (Joshua 6:5).

Abraham praised God *before* he ever saw Isaac (Romans 4:17).

If you will do the checking, you will find where there has been a loose connection. With a minor adjustment, you will be on the road again.

God's Word never fails.

Man of faith, the Lord Jesus will never fail you. Put your unwavering confidence in Him. You will have victory every time!

Reflection from
JOEL

*M*ake no mistake about it, there will be opposition in your life; there will be weapons formed against you, and they may be formidable and frightening. You will not go under; you will go through. The Scripture says, "The righteous person may have many troubles, but the LORD delivers him from them all" (Psalm 34:19 NIV).

When things get tough or things don't go your way, keep your confidence up. The Bible says when you've done all you know how to do, just keep on standing strong. Keep praying, keep believing, keep singing songs of praise. Keep fighting the good fight of faith. If you do that, God promises to bring you out with the victory every time.

CHAPTER THIRTEEN

Jesus, *the* Author *and* Finisher *of* Our Faith

There is no limit to what a man of faith can do for God no matter where he is, if he will learn the basics of faith, dare to believe God, and act on His Word.

As I close this book, I want to remind you that faith is not something you *try* occasionally. Faith is not something you pull out of your back pocket in emergencies or during difficult times to try to make everything better. Many people teach about faith, but they never mention the Lord Jesus Christ, presenting faith as if it were a formula or a mechanical thing.

Faith is a way of life.

We read in Hebrews 12:1–2: "Therefore we also, since we are surrounded by so great a cloud of witnesses, let us lay aside every weight, and the sin which so easily ensnares us, and let us run with endurance the race that is set before us, *looking unto Jesus, the author and finisher of our faith,* who for the joy that was set before Him endured the cross, despising the shame, and has sat down at the right hand of the throne of God."

Faith has to do with a living Person, the Lord Jesus Christ.

Jesus is alive and doing very well. He is still the Lord of all creation. He is still the God of the whole universe. He still has all power and all authority in heaven and in earth.

Jesus is the Author and the Developer of our faith.

So . . . fellowship continually with the Lord Jesus. Be aware of His sweet presence in your daily life.

Love Him. Adore Him. Praise Him.

Take time to get with Jesus and let Him minister to you. Let Him teach you the Word of God.

"FOLLOW ME, AND I WILL MAKE YOU . . ."

Jesus said, "Follow Me, and I will make you fishers of men" (Matthew 4:19). *Living a life of faith is following Jesus.* It is not just being in a stationary, comfortable place where you can say to yourself, "I've got it made." As men of faith, we are continually subject to the call of the Master. He did not say to follow Him for a while and then sit down and stop following. Wherever Jesus goes and beckons you to follow Him, you should continue following Him.

There are great rewards when you follow Jesus. If you will follow Him, He will lead you where the fish are. He will lead you where the coin is in the fish's mouth. He will supply your needs. He will give you a life where His yoke is easy and His burden is light (Matthew 11:30).

Our responsibility as men of unwavering faith is to follow Jesus. You are not to make up your mind as to what you want to do and where you want to go. Follow Jesus as He directs! No matter what hardships you endure, Jesus walks the same path you are walking. He knows every crevice, every obstacle, and every blessing. Your part is to follow.

GOD HAS A PLACE CALLED *THERE* FOR YOU

We are living in a world filled with trouble, stress, and chaos. No doubt our days are similar to those we read about regarding the prophet Elijah whom we've studied extensively in this book. In 1 Kings 17, Elijah represents the man of faith who stood strong for God during a period of drought, great distress, and spiritual and social upheaval. It was of utmost importance that Elijah *listen* to God and do *exactly* what God told him to do. Our responsibility today is to tune our spirits to the Holy

Spirit, to listen to God, to do what He tells us to do, and go where He tells us to go. When we do these things, our needs will be supplied, and we will be safe!

Elijah drew aside from his daily routine and prayed. He sought God. It is important to get in touch with God, to hear from God. We need to get away from people. There is a time we need to draw away. People will confuse you and discourage you. They will talk about other people. They will drag your faith down many times. As Elijah did, sometimes you just have to get alone and climb the hill of God, above the fog and smog of this world. Wrap your fingers in the garments of God and say, "My Father, my Father, I will not let You go until You bless me!" We must seek God diligently and follow His direction for our lives.

Elijah heard the voice of God. "Then the word of the LORD came to him, saying . . ." (1 Kings 17:2–4). Now God told him where to go and what to do. He said, "Get away from here and turn eastward, and hide by the Brook Cherith, which flows into the Jordan. And it will be that you shall drink from the brook, and I have commanded the ravens to feed you *there*."

God can tell you where to go. He has a *place* called *there* for you. That place called *there* is where God said, "I have commanded the ravens to feed you." If you are

Wrap yourself up in your devotion to Him. Make Him first in your life, and go where He directs you.

not in that place called *there*, you will be missing out on the fullness of God's blessing in your life.

In my own life, God sent me back to pastor Lakewood Church from the Philippine Islands in 1969. At that time, I did not want to come because I had been traveling all over the world preaching the Gospel. But you see, Lakewood Church was my place called *there*. If I had said, "No, I'm not going to go," I would have been in a mess, because this is where He called me to follow Him.

I believe there is a place called *there* for every believer. That does not mean there will never be battles to fight. That does not mean you are not going to face some tests and trials. But when you are in your *there*, you can enter into God's peace and rest. When you are in the place called *there*, the ravens will come and there will be ample provision and blessing.

Major on loving Jesus. Wrap yourself up in your devotion to Him. Make Him first in your life, and go where He directs you. Go to that place called *there*, and He can provide for your every need as He directs! God has unlimited resources for you.

KEEP FOLLOWING JESUS

Just because God sends you to one place does not mean you are going to stay there forever. Regarding Elijah, he "went and did according to the word of the LORD, for he went and stayed by the Brook Cherith, which flows into the Jordan. The ravens brought him bread and meat in the morning, and bread and meat in the evening; and he drank from the brook. And it happened after a while that the brook dried up, because there had been no rain in the land" (vv. 5–7).

There are times when God wants you to move on. Do not try to stay when your brook dries up. *God is not going to do everything in the same way throughout your life.* If your brook dries up and just suddenly everything goes wrong, examine yourself. Go before God and say, "God, are You through with me here? Are You trying to tell me something?"

God had a new *there* for Elijah. "Then the word of the LORD came to him, saying, "Arise, go to Zarephath, which belongs to Sidon, and dwell *there*" (vv. 8–9). On this occasion, in the midst of the great calamity of that day, God used a widow to provide miraculously for Elijah, and throughout the time of famine God provided for every need. If you are in the place called *there*, where Jesus has sent you, He will sustain you.

Seek God. Know with assurance that you are in that place called *there*. God will then cause your every need to be met, and you will blossom into the fullness of your potential as a man of unwavering faith.

MAKE THIS YOUR PRAYER

"Father, in Jesus' Name I seek Your divine guidance for my life. I thank You that Jesus lives in me, and the Bible says that He is made to me wisdom. You told me that if I lack wisdom, I should ask You, and You would supply me with all wisdom for every situation liberally. As I now ask You, I thank You, Father, that from this time forward You are supplying me with the wisdom that I need.

"I am Your sheep, and I do hear Your voice, and no other voice will I follow. I trust in You, Lord, with all my heart, and I do not lean on my own understanding. I acknowledge You in all my ways, and I know that You are directing my path. I follow the way of peace, for Jesus, the Prince of Peace, lives within me.

"Your Word is a lamp unto my feet and a light unto

my path. As I read and meditate on Your Word, You will speak to me. I thank You, Father, that the Holy Spirit lives within me and He will guide me into all Truth. He will not guide me into error, but only into truth and good. My spirit does bear witness with the Holy Spirit, confirming the will of God for my life.

"I take a stand against confusion or frustration, and I boldly declare that I will rest in Your love. I commit myself to follow You wherever You lead, Jesus. Thank You, Lord, for keeping me in Your perfect way! Amen."

FAITH HAS TO DO WITH A LIVING PERSON,

the Lord Jesus Christ.

Reflection from
JOEL

You *may have received a bad report from the doctor. Maybe you lost your largest client at work. Perhaps you just found out that your child is in trouble. You may be facing some other serious setback, and you feel as though life has caved in on top of you, knocking you off your feet and pushing you into the pits. You may be in a situation today where you have done your best. You've prayed and believed. You've placed your faith firmly on the truth of God's Word. But it just doesn't look like anything good is happening. Now you're tempted to say, "What's the use? It's never going to change."*

Don't give up! Keep standing. Keep praying; keep believing; keep hoping in faith. "Seek the LORD and His strength; seek His face evermore!" (Psalm 105:4).